JULIE D. ELLINGTON

WARRIORS IN TRAINING

FIGHTING YOUR BATTLES GOD'S WAY

Published by hope*books
2217 Matthews Township Pkwy
Suite D302
Matthews, NC 28105
www.hopebooks.com

hope*books is a division of hope*media

Printed in the United States of America

First paperback edition.
Paperback ISBN: 979-8-89185-228-0
Hardcover ISBN: 979-8-89185-229-7
Ebook ISBN: 979-8-89185-230-3
Library of Congress Number: 2025937977

hb
hope*books

Dedication

To my mother, my father, and my sister—

for believing I could write this book, even when I struggled.

To my mother, who once asked me, during a hard moment,

"Have you read your own book?"

In loving memory of my father, William "Duke" Ellington.

CONTENTS

CHAPTER 1: Introduction 1

CHAPTER 2: Recognize the Battlefield 9

CHAPTER 3: Understand the Opponents 27

CHAPTER 4: Expose Enemy Tactics 45

CHAPTER 5: Identify the Battle 67

CHAPTER 6: Preparing for Battle 85

CHAPTER 7: Equip for Battle 99

CHAPTER 8: Stand Firm 121

CHAPTER 9: Continue God's Call 137

CHAPTER 10: Conclusion 151

CHAPTER 1

INTRODUCTION

In all honesty and transparency, I did not want to pray for this person. They kept popping into my thoughts while I was praying, and I stubbornly pushed them right back out. But I could feel the nudging by the Holy Spirit, and with a sigh, I agreed to pray. I thought that maybe I would provide just a few mentions while I was asking for others, especially since I felt abandoned by them. I told myself, this was no big deal, I can do this, I must be obedient to the Holy Spirit, or He will stop giving me nudges.

I didn't think more about it until the struggle began.

But wait, I did not ask for this battle. For the record, I didn't even want to pray for them.

As I stumbled forward with interceding for this person, I realized that my situation was not uncommon. I could not be the only one experiencing this. Many of us find ourselves caught in a struggle we were not expecting after we agreed to pray, or agreed to help in ministry, or agreed to answer a call we believed was from the Lord.

The circumstances look far from where they originally started, and our expectations and hopes begin to crumble. The list of opposition grows along with the questions and doubts, and we become discouraged. We are ready to quit, unsure of how we found ourselves in this sticky mess that did not present itself as a possible cost in our estimation.

Months of praying for this person here and there landed me not only fighting for them, but for my own faith, my own trust in God. The battle just kept snowballing into more battles on more fronts. I was shocked by the hornet's nest that began to swarm around me. I don't remember kicking one. I can't remember much of the beginning details because I was caught off guard. This was another request for someone on my prayer list. I didn't even notice right away until the confusing thoughts and ideas started to actually sting.

Was I consistent and diligent in praying for this person? No. They had hurt me, pushed me out of their life, and I stayed away from them. So when I started feeling nudges to pray for them, I wasn't excited. I would reluctantly pray, just to acknowledge the push. And then I would get third-hand news, which went exactly against what I was praying for. So, I would cry out to God, "Why am I bothering with this? I didn't even want to pray for them in the first place, and now this isn't even working!" The cycle became laughable. I would pray, I would get news, I would throw up my hands in exasperation, I would stop. I would begin to think I was getting even the nudges wrong, and think *it has to be me that is misunderstanding,* and I would stop. There would be silence and calm. Some time would go by, and I would perceive the question, "Why aren't you praying? I've told you to pray." I would pray… This went on for over two years.

At first, the prayers were over matters of concern about the reckless choices this person was making. Then one reckless choice led to a bigger, unwise choice on their part, and the choices steadily got bigger and more serious. Towards the end of the two years, I was praying for their very life.

I learned so many lessons during that battle of intercession. I realized that what I went through during that time, I had gone through before, but overlooked completely. But this time, I was in a different spiritual place and knew more than I had in the past. Now, I was so much more aware of flaming arrows aimed at me. So often, at the beginning of the battle, my thoughts were, "Wait, what was that? Was that aimed at me directly? That really hurt! Why am I getting all this noise?"

I have had many different professions, but currently, I am a certified teacher. The teacher in me wanted to share these lessons with you. There is so much to include and say about the battles we face and their scope that I am unable to cover it all. I want you to have the insights I received to help ease the burden of being in a fight. The battle that started the writing of this book was my intercession for someone's life, but battles cover our ministries, our prayer lives, our families, and our witness to others. What I learned can be applied to all we have battles over.

My prayer and hope is to encourage you and cheer for you as we battle on for the Lord in the same army.

Even writing this book about fighting battles was a battle. I can't tell you how many times I wanted to quit writing. I had hit walls and gotten overwhelmed by all I wanted to say. I wanted to write fluently and clearly, but my sentences were confusing and choppy. I had to turn to the Lord during these times when I was relying on my own strength and ran my cart into the ditch. I would calmly wait, or sometimes not so calmly tell Him why I was frustrated. He always led me to the next step or the next insight.

Will I have answers for all of your questions? No, I will point you to the One who does. Almost every chapter is preparation and training that we cannot do on our own, and for which we must receive help and insight from God. I am only passing on what I have learned and been given, and I pray that the lessons will be helpful for you. If they don't connect directly with what you are facing, maybe they can lead you to a verse or a prayer that will prepare and train you to be His soldier and warrior.

Throughout the Bible, we have so many warriors who struggled in the midst of the battle. Their struggles during their physical and spiritual battles bring us encouragement and guidance. Throughout this book, we will be gleaning these scriptures for how God's warriors handled and trained for battle. We will look at such warriors as King David and the prophet Elijah. Both David and Elijah are being hunted by evil, hiding in the wilderness to continue the mission God had given them to do. God is so gentle with both of these men in their quest to live and obey Him, answering their questions and encouraging them as they figure things out. He will do the same for us.

There are two lessons right away to realize: We are not left alone, and our battle has the same plot, just different settings. This is not in vain, and our battle is never for nothing.

Paul is another warrior we can learn from. In 2 Corinthians 11:22–30, Paul gives a rundown of all the opposition he faced in spreading the gospel. In this passage, he reluctantly admits to all his hard work, his frequent prison stays, his beatings, and being near death again and again. He reveals he was flogged five times, beaten with rods three times, stoned once, shipwrecked three times, and survived in the deep one day and night. He was constantly moving, in danger of rivers and bandits and fellow Jews and Gentiles. He was in danger in the city, in the country, at sea, and in danger from false believers. He faced hardships and toiled often with no sleep, no food, in hunger and thirst, while cold and exposed. Paul was met with opposition that many of us will never see. But he was not taken down in all of those trials and tribulations. He was protected by God and triumphed with Jesus until he surrendered to Rome. In prison, he wrote the letters that make up so much of the New Testament that still lead us today.

Breaking down our battles into parts is not like sorting them into their proper categories, like puzzle pieces.

Instead, the parts are entwined and overlap into confusing chaos. But here we go, dissecting and pulling apart in order to help and encourage with continuing the fight. Remember, your fight is for something.

I feel I must include that I do not believe that the way to stop these attacks is by being more knowledgeable. There have been situations that I have analyzed to the point of powder, and even then, I had no better understanding than before. I believe the attacks will not stop as long as we are working and serving the Lord. I do believe that knowing what to look for and being more prepared might take the edge off the arrow aimed at our trust. We might not be so rocked and teetering on forsaking God, mad and disillusioned.

As part of studying the Bible and writing this book, I have done verse mapping and homiletics on the passages I included as well as read several commentaries—Matthew Henry, who is early 1700's Presbyterian; Benson, who is late 1700's Methodist; MacLaren, who is 1800's Scottish Baptist; and Ellicott, who is 1800's Church of England. I am a learner and a teacher. I love to learn and hear other perspectives. I quote different authors and scholars, both dead and living at the time I am writing; they each write from a different time, but offer such insight. You will see a wide collection of commentaries with a few secular quotes, because battle is battle. They wrote to help us, and they helped me. And I give you quotes to make you aware of others' encouragement and help. I hope you will check their God-given wisdom and insight more in your studies.

My goal for this book is to encourage and support you in your struggles and wrestling. Our physical and spiritual battles are urgent and wearying and have the capacity to destroy relationships and more. If anything I was given and learned can help you as you fight, then I will have my prayers answered.

PRAYER

Our Father, help us to keep our focus on You as we face the battles in our lives. May we draw closer to You and not turn away because of these struggles. Our desire is not to find answers without You or outside of You, but to learn the lessons You are longing to teach us. We look to You for wisdom, discernment, comfort, strength, and courage, knowing You will provide these and more.

CHAPTER 2

RECOGNIZE THE BATTLEFIELD

Months passed before the realization dawned on me that by agreeing to pray, I had enlisted myself into the armed forces. I started by praying what I felt the Holy Spirit prompted me to pray. There should be no problems with that, right? I was just obeying orders. I would intercede for this person to be saved from the current situation they led themselves into, and then go on about my business with no fuss or drama. This was stress-free praying until the confusing questions and negative statements began to swirl around my head and heart. These murmurings invaded my thoughts and feelings, and I began to doubt if I had even had these nudges from the Holy Spirit. I'd be doing something mindless, such as washing dishes or trying to fall asleep, and a thought would spring into my head, ripping open old but barely healed insecurity wounds. Thoughts that questioned my worth: *Who was I to ask for such things*, and *remember what happened the last time you prayed?* Thoughts that subtly reminded me how none of my prayers were answered before, and there was really no use because people are going to do what they want to do. Thoughts that urged that prayers don't change anything, and therefore, my prayers wouldn't matter. The more frequently these thoughts buzzed around me, the more I wondered if this is what stepping on a landmine would be like. Taking step after step, and then an explosion surrounds you, leaving you disoriented and injured. I know in my head what prayer can be and what prayer can do, but did I fully understand what I was starting?

The more I thought about the landmine analogy, the more I questioned, Aren't landmines installed on battlefields? Since when did I walk onto a battlefield littered with landmines? Just where did this landmine come from? Who placed these landmines and why? I had become a participant in a battle immensely larger than me.

An Act of War

According to the International Campaign to Ban Landmines website, landmines are put on battlefields to cause destruction, to maim, and stop a soldier from advancing. They are concealed under the ground or camouflaged. Landmines are "used defensively, to protect strategic areas such as borders, camps, or important bridges and to restrict the movement of opposing forces."[1]

1 International Campaign to Ban Landmines. *A History of Landmines*. icblcmc, 2 Sept. 2023, https://icblcmc.org/our-impact/a-history-of-landmines. Accessed 31 July 2024.

Using that definition, landmines are an indicator that we are approaching an area the enemy doesn't want us near. I once heard a gamer explain that he knew he was heading in the right direction in a video game when he started encountering enemies. Landmines and hidden traps should be viewed with the understanding that the enemy wants us to stop where we are headed. Our approach to territory controlled by our enemies is an act of war. Prayers and ministries that march against what the enemy is doing or has under his control in personal lives or in cities and countries are aggressive attacks and will be dealt with as such. We have crossed a borderline and picked a fight with the landlord.

Do we realize that is what is happening? Do we think much about the ground we walk on? I confess that I did not give any thought to the land until I began to analyze the spiritual battle I found myself in the middle of. Is the ground given any importance in our lives? We notice and enjoy it; many of us buy and own it, and some of us farm and use it. The ground has been and will be there tomorrow. I have taken the ground for granted my whole life, and that is my own fault. Maybe there were sermons preached and writings explaining this importance, but I failed to take notice. So I scrambled to realize where I was standing until, after the warning shots were fired my way.

On the other hand, bits and pieces of this earth have been the object of wars since the fall in Genesis 3. Battles have been raging over borders, countries, and territories throughout history. The ground we take for granted has been fought over and bled on. Archaeologists have discovered that the ground harbors secrets and treasures. Always in the backdrop but never the star of the show. But the ground is God's creation, and He gave it a vital role in the environment He gave us. Have we paid attention to how much this land means to God?

The physical world parallels the spiritual world, and through analysis, this parallel can help us improve our understanding of the spiritual realm. Review of what Scripture says about physical land can give us more insight into our spiritual battles. If we give little notice to the physical ground we are standing on when we are fighting in the middle of our battles, we most likely overlook the importance of the spiritual ground as we struggle to contend in spiritual matters. Studying several Old Testament passages as well as the New Testament, we can grasp more about the spiritual ground our spiritual battle is raging over.

Creation of Dry Ground

To show the importance of the land, we will start with Genesis chapter 1, where God creates physical dry ground on the third day. The dry land appears before both animals and humans. God makes man from the dust of the earth three days later and directs man to fill the earth and subdue it. The land was to provide for all of God's creations, and man was given the task to work it. Verses 29 and 30 talk about how the earth provided food for all the creatures on the ground. So before the fall, all animals were sustained by the earth itself, not each other. The food chain was not necessary because the Earth was designed to sustain all life. The fall of man in chapter 3 brings curses to not only man and woman, but the land and the animals as well.

God proclaims, "...Cursed is the ground because of you; through painful toil you will eat food from it all the days of your life. It will produce thorns and thistles for you, and you will eat the plants of the field. By the sweat of your brow you will eat your food until you return to the ground, since from it you were taken; for dust you are and to dust you will return" (Genesis 3:17–19, NIV). Now, because man chose sin, the ground is cursed and will be another source of labor and toil to man. When Adam and Eve surrender the land they were given, the battle over physical and spiritual territory heats up.

The land is not untouched by this surrender. Not long after the fall, humans began to increase in number, along with wickedness. Genesis 6 tells us that God mourned and judged all creation as humans lost sight of their created design. The humans were unaware of and unconcerned with their sin against God. The physical implications of their sin affected the physical ground and caused it to become spiritually cursed. The earth's inhabitants had become corrupt in God's view, and He purified the land of man and all of man's works by flooding it with water. Both land and animals paid part of the price by being overcome by water. The Earth's dynamics were changed forever in order to cleanse God's ground.

Land is Promised by God

The earth is populated once again, and God calls a descendant of Noah's blessed son, Shem, to go to a place God will show him. Jumping to chapter 12 of Genesis, God shows this descendant of Shem, Abram (later named Abraham), a parcel of land and promises to give this to him and his offspring. God's promise of land is a gift. The Bible does not say that Abraham had asked for this. Verse 7 of this chapter states, "The LORD appeared to Abram and said, 'To your descendants I will give this land.' So he built an altar to the LORD, who had appeared to him" (Genesis 12:7, NASB, 1995 ed.). This promise is reaffirmed by God in Genesis 15:18 and again in Genesis 17:8. Abraham did not earn this promised land from God, just as we cannot earn the promised land of eternity with God.

Centuries later, Abraham's family has multiplied and has relocated from the area to Egypt to survive a drought. After living in Egypt for around four hundred years, the time has come for God's people to take possession of the land He promised them as descendants of Abraham. Chapter 13 of of Numbers has the LORD telling the leader, Moses, to "send men to spy out the land of Canaan which I am giving to the children of Israel." This very ground was promised by the Promise Keeper to Abraham and the Israelites hundreds of years before, and now the promise is being fulfilled. The battles for them to possess this land God promised to them were many and stretched out over decades.

Battlegrounds

Now that we have reviewed how important the physical ground can be, we can look at the parallels between physical and spiritual ground. Just as one can advance ground, defend ground, and lose ground, we can also advance spiritual ground, defend our spiritual ground, lose spiritual ground, and reject ground. As we advance the kingdom of God on earth, we are given the task to gain ground. We also defend the ground we were given, as the enemy is constantly looking for and creating opportunities to steal. Both involve fighting, battles, and wars. And of course, spiritual ground can always be lost, and sometimes, there isn't even a battle; we surrender and hand it over.

Battles in this world and time are not a fight and win to never fight again. We will always be fighting, and we will always be in training. We can either learn how to be better at battle and become warriors, or we can stop and quit. We will not always be in just one category, but we will be moving from one to the other as the battle rages. This learning process can become a cycle resembling the Israelites throughout the book of Judges. They would gain the Promised Land, they would lose the land to their enemies, they would give up and let their enemies oppress them, they would fight their enemies to regain the land, they would gain the land again. And repeat. We are the same as the Israelites. We can have victory on one front while losing on another.

Advancing Ground

Advancing the territory of God is not just recruiting more members on God's side. The saving of souls is part of this, but the preparation and tilling of the ground for these souls to receive Christ is also progress. The ground we reference can be our hearts and lives, with the removal of sinful natures to become more like Christ. The ground can be prepared for the growth and production of the fruit of the Spirit listed in Galatians 5:22–23. The growth of love, joy, peace, patience, kindness, goodness, faithfulness, gentleness, and self-control is ground that is gained. When the presence of hate, anger, impatience, selfishness, evil, adultery, violence, and indiscipline is retreating, the enemy is losing ground and the kingdom of God is proceeding.

We worry about measurement and time, but God does not concern Himself with these like we do. Luke 13 tells of Jesus teaching what the kingdom of God is like. He uses two parables to illustrate. One parable is a tiny mustard seed that grows into an enormous tree, quietly and slowly. The second parable is that His kingdom is like a small amount of yeast silently working until it has spread throughout the dough (Luke 13:18–21). God's timing is not our timing, and God's ways are not our ways. We must not let others pressure us into counting and comparison and rushing when that is not God's way.

The enemy wants to keep the ground he has. He will not give it back without a colossal battle, and he will make such a theatrical fuss that we get scared or tired or worn out and we quit. Take, for instance, the battle of the Israelites to leave the land of being oppressed and enslaved by their enemy and occupy their Promised Land. And the land God had promised them had to be sanctified from the cursed ground of their enemies into hallowed land. The enemy did not lose without a massive fight and took several souls with him in the process. Another example is in the book of The Acts of the Apostles, which is filled with the struggles and trials the apostles dealt with to advance the new kingdom with the Good News of Jesus Christ. Here again, they tread on enemy ground and turned it into hallowed land. There were numerous battles the Apostles and Paul fought to gain ground for God's kingdom. God was with them, the Spirit guiding them every second of the way.

Wars, battles, and conflicts are all the Lord's, but God allows us to be involved and help with advancing His kingdom. Saving people from a spiritual death will be a raging war that will continue until the end of this heaven and earth. Attempting to change a person's path from eternal death to eternal life is viewed as treading on territory already marked for destruction. Wars we know nothing about are fought by the angel armies over gaining spiritual ground. Sending missionaries into regions of the world that have not heard of Jesus Christ and the gospel is expanding God's territory, but so is sharing the gospel with the person next to you, right where you have been planted. We can move forward anywhere. The ground is ripe for harvest.

Advancing ground is a cause for celebration. The parables Jesus tells in Luke 15 (NIV) give the picture of finding what was lost and rejoicing when it's found. The three parables are very similar, but each has a slight difference in detail. The first parable is The Lost Sheep, given in verses 1–7, where the shepherd leaves the other sheep safe in the open country and goes looking for that one lost sheep. Verses 5–6 tell of the joy of finding the lost: "And when he finds it, he joyfully puts it on his shoulders and goes home. Then he calls his friends and neighbors together and says, 'Rejoice with me, I have found my lost sheep.'" The second parable of The Lost Coin in verses 8–10 is similar, but the woman brings light, sweeps the entire house, and searches diligently. Jesus says in verses 9–10, "And when she finds it, she calls her friends and neighbors together and says, 'Rejoice with me; I have found my lost coin.' In the same way, I tell you, there is rejoicing in the presence of the angels of God over one sinner who repents."

The third parable, The Prodigal Son, is given in verses 11–32. The father reacts differently and does not go searching for his lost son. He waits for the son to return, and the son does. The father has to defend the enormous and extravagant party that he throws for his older son when the younger son returns in verse 32: "But we had to celebrate and be glad, because this brother of yours was dead and is alive again; he was lost and is found."

Maybe part of our battle in advancing ground is discerning and seeking which way God would have us go. Maybe God wants us to actively go out and search, or maybe we are directed to light lamps and sweep the ground we've been given. Maybe we wait, not rushing or pushing, for God to do the work. In each parable, the story is told about finding one. One at a time. One fight, one conflict, one battle at a time. One is enough to throw parties for. We can wrestle with measuring, comparison, and fretting over progress and measurements when heaven celebrates over one. We can be happy and rejoice as we watch things grow and progress.

Defending Ground

Ephesians 4:27 (NIV) states, "and do not give the devil a foothold." The definition for foothold is a place for which the foot can rest securely. Another definition is a secure, strategic position from which one can advance.[2] One source states: "In World War II, Allied forces invaded Normandy, France, and established a beachhold—a foothold—behind enemy lines. That foothold allowed the Allies to create a base of operations and proved to be a springboard to victory in Europe.[3] Both sides of the battle can use footholds to gain ground. However, we have an enemy that is always looking for a way to get us to fall and lose ground to him. If the land is God-given, your enemy wants it. Why? To take God's glory, to give away God's promise and God's Word, to tarnish God's name, to show

2 *Funk & Wagnalls Standard College Dictionary*. Funk & Wagnalls, 1980.

3 "What Is a Foothold?" *Got Questions?*, https://www.gotquestions.org/what-is-a-foothold.html. Accessed June 30, 2025.

that God cannot be trusted and cannot keep promises. This list is not exhaustive.

An example of defending ground is found in Matthew 4:1–11, where the devil tries to tempt Jesus. The devil takes Jesus to a high mountain and offers to give Jesus all the land and kingdoms of the world He sees. This parallels the passage in Genesis 13:14–17, where God takes Abraham to a high mountain and promises to give him all that Abram can see. Except in Genesis 13, the land is God's to give to whomever He pleases. The devil tries to entice Jesus to worship him by promising to give Jesus all the land Jesus can see. Except, it's not the devil's to give.

Jesus was given spiritual ground right before He was led into the desert to be tempted. In Matthew 4:1–10, He defended this ground with verses from Deuteronomy, cementing His worship and faithfulness to His Father alone. The devil tempts Jesus with bluffs, lies, and twisted Scripture. Jesus responds by directing. The devil tempts Jesus to turn rocks into bread, but in John 6:35, Jesus says that He is the bread of life. The devil tempts Jesus to throw himself off the temple, but in John 2:19–21 (NIV), Jesus says, "Destroy this temple, and I will raise it again in three days," referring to his body as the Temple. Jesus is the temple. The devil tempts Jesus with all the kingdoms of the world and their splendor if Jesus will bow down and worship him, but in John 10:30, Jesus says, "I and the Father are one." All these things that the devil tempted Jesus with, Jesus was himself. This should be an encouragement, for if the devil does that with Jesus, who created all things and is all things, we can guarantee that's how he will tempt us.

Losing Ground

We are very capable of losing the ground that has been fought for and given to us. In the beginning of Genesis 3, Adam and Eve lose their physical as well as spiritual ground. They were given the physical land with the Garden of Eden and the spiritual land of direct communication and relationship with God. But they chose something other than belief and trust in God, and they were removed forever from the garden. Not only were they kept out of the Garden of Eden, but the ground they were given to live on was cursed by their choice, too. Spiritual ground was lost as their relationship with God changed, and death, both a physical death and a spiritual death, was made a consequence.

Deuteronomy chapters 28 and 29 warn the Israelites, upon entering the Promised Land, that if they follow God, they can keep the land. If they forsake God, they lose the land. Verses 23–28 of chapter 29 detail how their disobedience would affect the land God gave them with disease and barrenness. The Israelites continue to lose this land to their enemies over and over again in the book of Judges. After a war to win the Promised Land, the Israelites finally occupy it, only to lose it to their adversaries. All the warnings clearly stated in Deuteronomy 28 and 29 happen in Judges due to their worship of other gods and their disobedience to the One True God. The Israelites get in this cycle where they win and then lose their land to their enemies. They refuse to remain faithful to God and continue to fall into oppression by their physical and spiritual enemies.

Both of these examples are about losing ground due to our own choices and our own disobedience to God and God alone. But ground can be lost due to others' choices and others' disobedience beyond our control. To name a few: churches split, marriages crumble, children walk away from the faith they were raised in, missionaries leave, and apathy sets in.

Refusing Ground

The last possibility concerning a battle for spiritual land can be found in Numbers 13 (NIV). The first two verses of this chapter are God telling Moses, "Send some men to explore the land of Canaan, which I am giving to the Israelites. From each ancestral tribe send one of its leaders." The Israelites are being prepared to receive their promise. God wants to give His people the land, but His people struggle to trust Him to receive it. Verses 28–29 tell of the spies' return, and ten of the twelve spies focus on the problems: "But the people who live there are powerful, and the cities are fortified and very large. We even saw descendants of Anak there. The Amalekites live in the Negev; the Hittites, Jebusites, and Amorites live in the hill country; and the Canaanites live near the sea and along the Jordan." The ten fueled the people's fear and inflamed the tribes into grumbling against Moses and Aaron with the intent of choosing their own leaders to return to Egypt in Numbers 14:1-4. The Israelites' response to God's direction was rejection of God's promise. They believed there was no way they could do what God had told them to do, and they gave up. Not only did they want to quit moving forward, but they also wanted to go back to their slavery. They not only squander their time and chance to move into this land, but God judges them and causes them to wander the wilderness for forty years until this generation dies. Look at all they lost because they couldn't trust the LORD. They lost everything and never saw the Promised Land again. Let us learn from this lesson not to do the same.

Training

How can we prepare and train for battle by knowing what ground we are given? I believe this can help us focus on what to do instead of just trying to stop the landmines from blowing up around us by whatever means necessary. If we are confused and disoriented, many of us will quit. I wanted to and did for a bit. I chose flight instead of fight many times. It can also help us to expect pushback when we begin something and not be discouraged because we believe we've done the wrong thing.

These are all part of working on a better relationship with the Father, the Son and the Holy Spirit. None of this should be attempted without Him. We must be in connection with the Holy Spirit in prayer and be able to discern what we are being led to do. If we feel we are to advance and start crossing into enemy territory, what way does the Holy Spirit want us to proceed? We looked at three possibilities such as going out and searching, staying where you are and searching, and staying where you are and allowing the advancement to be brought to you.

If we detect attacks and must defend the given land, we must study and know the Bible. Ask the Spirit where He wants you to start or where He wants you to improve. There are so many resources available, and you must not let feeling awkward stop you. Everyone, including scholars and experts, had to begin somewhere. No one arrives at the point where they know it all, and everyone continues to learn about God, Jesus, the Holy Spirit, and the Word of God.

If we feel we are losing ground, first, we should repent of our own sins. No one is without sin, and many times, we are blind to our own. The less obvious sins, such as distrust in God, white lies, people-pleasing, and holding grudges, are still sins. Ask the Holy Spirit to help you see what sin and temptation need to be removed from your heart and life. Ask if you have any idols that need to be identified and removed because they lead you to worship other things and ideas instead of God. This part will hurt your feelings. Prepare for that. Once we've checked for our responsibility in the situation, we can intercede for others and their decisions.

Pray that you would be open to the conviction of the Holy Spirit, where unbelief and distrust of God have you refusing to move forward with what He has told you to do. Ask the Holy Spirit to show why there is unbelief and a lack of trust on your part. I've been convicted of this and was shown exactly why and in what area of my life. When I asked this question, I was shown immediately. This can open old wounds, so do this with the protection of prayer. This needs to be addressed and worked on directly. From what we reviewed in Numbers 13 and my own experience, God does not take being distrusted well.

Establishing what ground we are fighting for can be a process. Do not give up, as it feels awkward to ask questions and figure this out. You might not be sure what your fight is even over. Below are some questions to think over or journal (my favorite).

What territory are you approaching that the enemy wants to stop you from what you are doing, and even better, remove you from the situation completely? When did the landmines and warning shots begin?

What ground have you been given by God? This could be a mission to go to a certain land or a certain place to serve Him. It doesn't have to be far away and can be as close as where you work or your neighborhood. Maybe it is a calling to go and do a certain job or task. Maybe He wants you to write or speak. Is it a prayer of intercession for someone? Your ground could be a promise, a word, or a verse that He has given you. You might feel you have no land given to you, but maybe you gave it away. Whatever your ground may be, we have caught the notice of the enemy, and we must train for battle.

PRAYER

Dear Jehovah, You are the Creator and Sustainer of our lives. If You have called us to fight, we need You and only You. Please give us Your insight and Your wisdom into training us to be better soldiers for You. Help our focus by showing us what ground we are standing on. We are unable to fight Your way without You. Please give us Scripture to light the ground we stand on and defend. Thank you for the wisdom and discernment that can only be trusted when given from You in Your Word. Your kingdom come, Your will be done, on earth as it is in heaven.

CHAPTER 3

UNDERSTAND THE OPPONENTS

We are offered the choice to follow Jesus Christ and conduct our lives His way. This is not one decision but a million little decisions. To follow Christ and abide His way would be like choosing a team. Therefore, the other teams are now our opponents because they were opponents of Jesus Christ first. Scripture gives us vital information about what we are up against, and we have more than one enemy.

If you have watched a movie about sports victories, there will likely be scenes where the team collectively reviews their opponent. They review the style and plays their competition uses, who to watch for, what to be on alert about, if they are tricky or violent, and how to react and counter. But this review of the opponents is certainly not to glorify them or a chance to join the opposing team. This is part of preparing and training for victory.

Not only do we have more than one enemy, we have

more than two. There is the one, the devil, and we will review his characteristics in the following paragraphs. Just as sure as we have an enemy outside of ourselves, we also have an enemy within ourselves. We have a choice to follow or not follow these selfish desires, but they do exist and work as an adversary. And if each of us has a will and a way of our own, that means that another person's will is not my advocate either. That makes three categories so far.

Enemy 1

As we discuss our first enemy, I do not want to focus or dwell on him other than to know about him and be aware of his mode of operation. However, so he doesn't get more attention than needed, I am going to contrast him to the One he is not. First and most important, he is not God or even on the same level as Jesus or the Holy Spirit. He is not omnipresent and can only be in one place at any given time. The devil is not omniscient and is not all-knowing, all-wise, and all-seeing as the Trinity is. He is limited by and under the authority of God and Jesus. However, he is supernatural, and we, on the human level, are no match for him. He is to be noted, but our focus needs to be on Jesus, not on our enemy. If we study too much, the devil will steal our focus as well. Jesus is God, the Son of God, and the devil is not. Therefore, he will never be Jesus's counterpart. Satan is a created being; Jesus always existed.

Characteristics

John 10:7–11 warns,

> "So Jesus again said to them, 'Truly, truly I say to you, I am the door of the sheep. All who came before me are thieves and robbers, but the sheep did not listen to them. I am the door. If anyone enters by me, he will be saved and will go in and out and find pasture. The thief comes only to steal and kill and destroy. I came that they may have life, and have it abundantly. I am the good shepherd. The good shepherd lays down his life for the sheep.'"

In these verses, Jesus assures His disciples several times that He is the good shepherd and gives His life for the sheep. Jesus comes so that they will have life and have life over and above what is necessary. Verse 10 contrasts the thief that only shows up to steal, kill, and destroy. This is the opposite of and adversarial to Jesus. The thief comes to steal what the good shepherd provides by stealth, rather than out in the open with violence. The opposite of giving life is killing, which means to slaughter. The devil feeds on destroying our relationship with God and Jesus. He is the adversary, the opposite, the opponent in almost everything he does. In the second sentence of John 10:10 (CSB), Jesus is saying, "I have come that they may have life and have it in abundance." The opposite of giving life is taking life; the opposite of giving abundant life is taking all life.

Jesus gives another warning concerning our enemy in

John 8:44 as he is speaking with the teachers of the law and the Pharisees, "You are of your father the devil, and your will is to do your father's desires. He was a murderer from the beginning, and does not stand in the truth, because there is no truth in him. When he lies, he speaks out of his own character, for he is a liar and the father of lies." While Jesus gives life, the devil destroys life. While Jesus is the truth, the devil is a liar. Jesus and the devil will never be on the same side. They will be polar opposites in everything, and we can use that in learning about our enemy and his tactics.

Wiles

The Apostle Paul advises in Ephesians 6:11–13 putting on the complete set of God's armor so that we may be able to stand against the wiles of the devil. I will review the pieces of armor in an upcoming chapter, but the word to center on right now for this passage is the word *wiles*. Synonyms for wiles include tricks, ruses, ploys, schemes, cunning, and subterfuges. The devil is a trickster. Jesus is straightforward, honest, and trustworthy, while the devil uses creative devices to deceive and destroy us.

The word "destroy" is being used and repeated as we talk about what the devil can do. What can the devil destroy exactly? When the serpent spoke with Eve in Genesis 3:4, he stated, "You will not surely die," and she did not die a physical death when she bit into the fruit. We must widen the definition and scope of what he and the evil forces are able to demolish. It might not be limited to the physical realm but also include the spiritual realm. Eve did not die physically the instant she disobeyed, but there was death in all she knew and loved, whether she perceived it or not. Evil can lead us to both a physical death and a spiritual death. He can keep us from our eternal spiritual life if we let him. If we believe and follow Jesus Christ, we will receive life for eternity. If we do not, we will receive a spiritual life that is destroyed forever. To be honest, sometimes, this destruction doesn't look bad. As we struggle and wrestle in our ministry and prayers, we can look around and see those who aren't following Jesus Christ, seeming to do better than we are. Psalm 73 voices this very idea.

The devil acts as a bully, puffing himself up to appear bigger and more powerful than he is, much like a predator animal does to its prey. He bluffs and puffs and badgers us around. In the future, if you study a passage with the devil or evil spirits included, notice their lies and theatrics fool us to believe they have more authority than they were given by God. Notice and note for future use.

Limits

The devil is given limited power and can only do so much. In the passage in Luke 10:18, Jesus recalls, "I saw Satan fall like lightning from heaven." We can conclude that because the devil is not omnipresent and can only be in one place at one time, the devil is bound to the Earth. Jesus calls the devil the prince of this world in John 14:30. This passage did not bring me comfort until I saw a video that compares the size of the Earth to the size of Saturn, Pluto, our Sun, our Solar System, and beyond. Have you seen a picture comparing the size of the Earth to the other planets and the Sun? It's minuscule. The Earth looks like a speck of dirt when compared to the size of other planets and the stars just in our solar system. God, Jesus, and the Holy Spirit are omnipresent in the entire universe, while the devil is the prince of his little speck of a kingdom. No wonder God doesn't find him a threat or get distraught over the devil's existence as we do. That is why I believe the devil bullies us. We are weaker and more limited than he is as a created supernatural being, and he knows that will hurt and distress God.

The devil has access to heaven, as shown in Job 1:6–12 and Job 2:1–2 when he is in the throne room of God, accusing Job of being all fluff and no substance. But in these passages, we are shown that God limits the devil in what he is allowed to do to Job.

We can say *no,* and he flees. James 4:7 (NLT) states, "So humble yourselves before God. Resist the devil, and he will flee from you." Limit him by saying *no*. Is he bothering you? No conversation is required or advised. Look what happened when Eve talked with the serpent. We are not better than Eve. "In the name of Jesus Christ, no. Leave." We are given that authority in Jesus' name.

Clarifications

There are a few ideas that are widely held about the devil, but after studying the Scriptures and some commentaries, I trust, I could not find that these ideas about the devil were based in Scripture. Please allow me to explain a possibility, as this information casts light on the monster in the dark corner of the room, which could expose him as just a blanket over a chair. He is our formidable foe, not God's, and we are told not to fear the devil. I hope the following paragraphs deflate the bully from his own aggrandizement.

In Hebrew culture, names are very significant and have meaning. Names are not given simply because the family likes it. The Israelites held names as the person's identity and the definition of who the person was. Abram had his name changed to Abraham, Jacob had his name changed to Israel, and Saul had his name changed to Paul. These names were changed by God, not the person. Names are important to God. That being said, in my studies of what the names Satan and Lucifer meant, I found commentaries that claimed those were not his name. What really caught my attention about this is watching a video from The Bible Project about the devil that explains that Satan is more of a title, and we should be putting "the" before the title.[4] There are titles and adjectives we use to identify him. We identify him as the devil, Satan, or even Lucifer. Jesus calls him Beelzebul in Matthew chapters 10 and 12. But look up the meaning in Hebrew for the Old Testament and Greek for the New Testament, and these names are defined as titles being used to identify the devil. To ex-

4 The Bible Project. "Who Is Satan and What Are Demons in the Bible?" *The Bible Project*, 23 May 2019, https://bibleproject.com/explore/video/satan-demons/. Accessed 31 July 2024.

plain using Hebrew names we know, we call Jesus by his name and add the title Christ. Or we call him Rabbi, but it's not his name. You also have John the Baptist. John is his name, and Baptist is what he does.

The fact that the name of the Satan, the adversary, is not given is a lowering of character and humbling. Even the animals were given names, as it was Adam's job to find names, as stated in Genesis 2. The devil is the slanderer, the false accuser, the adversary, the liar, the tempter. He is identified by what he is, not by a name. If our bully has been stripped of his name, how limited by God he must be!

Let me review with you what I found in my research into what these terms mean in the original Hebrew language, where they are found in the Bible. In accordance with Strong's Concordance, the Hebrew word for "devil" is *diabolos,* which means false accuser, slanderer.[5] *Thayer's Greek Lexicon* states the devil is "persecuting good men, estranging mankind from God, and enticing them to sin."[6] On the other hand, many of the sources I reviewed stated that Satan is another way of saying the devil. Strong's Concordance has the term "Satan" as *Satanas* and is defined as "the adversary." But we just say Satan, no name, just a title. We call him the devil, no name, just a generic title. His title used in Scripture will match what role he is playing at that time.

5 Strong, James. *Strong's Exhaustive Concordance of the Bible*. Abingdon Press, 1890.

6 Thayer, Joseph H. *Greek-English Lexicon of the New Testament*. Zondervan Publishing House, 1977.

There are other times when we use the name Lucifer, as found in Isaiah 14:12 (KJV) for the devil. Strong's Concordance defines the word "Lucifer" as *Helel,* which means "shining one." However, this source does not state Lucifer as a name for the adversary. The commentary of Charles John Ellicott explains this passage was misinterpreted many centuries ago in medieval Latin, and this name was mistakenly applied to the devil.[7] Verse 12 of Isaiah 14, although this parallels what we read about the devil, is addressed specifically to the king of Babylon. The newest revisions to NIV and ESV have totally removed the name Lucifer from this verse, and currently, the ESV verse reads as such: "How you are fallen from heaven, O Day Star, son of Dawn! How you are cut down to the ground, you who laid the nations low!"

Jesus refers to him in Matthew chapters 10 and 12 as Beelzebub, or Beelzebul. Strong's Concordance states this is another name for the devil; however, HELPS Word-Studies says this is a title for the devil and it stands for "the lord of the flies" or "fly-god".[8] *Thayer's Greek Lexicon* has this meaning: lord of dung or filth, the prince of evil spirits. Oh. Again, the use of the title to match the role the devil is playing at the time.

Another idea exposed is that there are spiritual forces other than the devil. I was under the impression that the

---

7 Ellicott, Charles John. *Isaiah 14 - Ellicott's Commentary for English Readers. Bible Hub,* 1905, https://biblehub.com/commentaries/ellicott/isaiah/14.htm. Accessed 4 Aug. 2025.

8 The Discovery Bible. "HELPS Word-studies." *The Discovery Bible,* 2020, http://thediscoverybible.com. Accessed 26 Apr. 2024.

devil was the chief commander over the dark forces, and they all answered to him. *Thayer's Greek Lexicon* cites that he is the prince of evil spirits. Therefore, I assumed he was leading the entire force. But the wording in Ephesians 6:12 (NKJV) has led me to think differently: "For we do not wrestle against flesh and blood, but against principalities, against powers, against rulers of the darkness of this age, against spiritual hosts of wickedness in heavenly places." We learn from this verse that there are rulers holding dominion entrusted to them in the order of things (principalities), authorities who are the more powerful among those created beings and are superior to men (powers). We also learn that there is a ruler of this world (the ruler of this darkness), and they all have access to the heavenly regions. Paul does not write that there is one, but it seems like there are several. If we are being harassed by evil, it's not going to be the devil himself. He's busy being in one place at one time.

I would think that because evil is the opposite of good and good is orderly and compliant, the evil forces would be the opposite. However, I am only doing so much research and not spending more time or focus to learn the hierarchy of the dark forces that oppose the kingdom of God. The information given is that these enemies are organized, they are watching us, and learning the best way to bring us down to stop us from spreading light in their dark territory. Let us be aware of these facts, but not let them interrupt us from being bold for our God, who is omniscient, omnipresent, infinite, mighty, and has a Name.

Our Responses

Scripture tells us that we are not to engage or worship the devil, fallen angels, evil armies, or evil spirits. In verse 11 of 2 Peter chapter 2, Peter states that angels, although they are stronger and more powerful, do not bring a reviling judgment against the fallen angels in the presence of the Lord. Jude 1:9 (NIV) discusses that even the archangel Michael did not dare to condemn the devil for slander as he was disputing with the devil over Moses' body. The fallen spiritual beings are more powerful than us, but we are not to be afraid of them. Even the devil, the adversary, is not on any level with Jesus, the Son of God. We must remember that the devil and the evil forces are limited by God and Jesus. We can turn to Jesus and say His Mighty Name when tempted or bothered by any evil force. Our fear and reverence is to be of the LORD.

I encountered the presence of evil spirits when I lived in Mzuzu, Malawi, Africa. The property where I lived was right next door to a witch doctor. I never saw him, but I would see his children out playing in their yard. We had a chain link fence running around the property, and we had a walking path right inside that fence. On my walks, I would walk past his property, and the darkness radiating from his compound gave me chills. I used to say Jesus' name with every step as I walked the ground next to him to keep back that darkness. Some nights, deep into the night, we could hear the drums from his property being played in rituals to bring up the dead. We would pray and repeat Jesus' name during those seances. After I moved out of Malawi, I was told he eventually relocated away from the property.

In the same African country of Malawi, my coworker came back from church one Sunday with a story about evil spirits. She and many others were called to pray over a group of school girls who loudly walked into their church, dancing boldly and irreverently to the worship music. Her friends asked for her help in praying, and they laid hands on the girls and prayed over them in Jesus' name for over half an hour before the spirits left them.

There is no doubt in my mind about the presence of enemy armies. They made no effort to disguise themselves in those rural areas. When I lived just outside of Nairobi, Kenya, the enemy was less obvious than in Malawi, but their presence was still there. Here in the United States, I find them even less obvious. Maybe with all our distractions and little self-built kingdoms and worries, the enemy doesn't have to work hard to deflect our attentiveness.

Enemy 2

We have several enemies, not just one. We have a significant enemy in the devil and all the evil forces. However, we have an enemy we live with constantly in our own selfish desires and arrogant will. Sometimes, our own will betrays us, and the evil forces and spirits don't have to even participate. I think the two work together in a horrible and fierce partnership and use each other to work against the kingdom of God.

During my time in Kenya, we were teaching the children about Adam and Eve's choice and all the consequences that choice brought and meant. No turning back or redos. A girl of thirteen years old piped up, asking for clarification, "So we have all this pain because of Eve?" "Well, yes," was the reply. "I hate Eve!" she said through clenched teeth. I can relate to her statement; however, we can blame Eve all we want, but we have the same will inside each of us.

Paul discussed the sin within each of us in several of his letters to the growing Christian church. Romans 7:15–16 is where Paul says, "I do not understand my own actions. For I do not do what I want, but I do the very thing I hate. Now if I do what I do not want, I agree to the Law that it is good." Paul does not put the blame on the devil or on evil forces. We have no excuse and we should take responsibility for our sin and not always blame it on the devil leading us into temptation. Yes, the devil has his ways and schemes but we choose to follow him, many times with our eyes wide open.

From the book *The Christian Warfare*, D. Martyn Lloyd-Jones states in chapter 24, "Self":

> According to the teaching of the Bible, self is responsible for all sin. The first 'fall' in God's creation was the fall of the devil... But he fell because of pride, which is nothing but a manifestation of self... The whole of evil ultimately emanates from this fact that self is present even in an angelic, a seraphic being, self was the cause of the downfall, that pre-cosmic fall that has led to the whole prob-

> lem of sin and evil...And the cause of man's failure was but a repetition of what had been true in the case of the devil. The devil knew the line he must adopt; he knew the very thing that was likely to ensnare the man and the woman... He played on pride, he played on self... It should not surprise us, therefore, that the devil in his wiliness constantly plays upon the particular aspect of our personality... The devil is still at work and with his wiles, he knows how to play upon our greatest weakness, which is self.[9]

There are so many verses to include to support that we have our own adversary within, even after we are saved. We think that when we become Christians, the self-centeredness disappears, and then we are shocked when we realize how our wills were used. In Jeremiah 2:13 (NIV), the LORD states, "My people have committed two sins: they have forsaken me, the spring of the living water and have dug their own cisterns, broken cisterns that cannot hold water." Notice what this passage does not say—My people have committed sins: they followed the devil and he made them sin. No, we dug our own well and got our water our own way. Another verse is Colossians 2:13 (NLT), where Paul states, "You were dead because of your sins and because your sinful nature was not yet cut away. Then God made you alive with Christ, for he forgave all our sins." Paul puts the responsibility of sin directly on

9 Lloyd-Jones, D. Martyn. *The Christian Warfare: An Exposition of Ephesians 6:10–13.* Baker Publishing Group, 1998.

our shoulders and does not pass it off to our adversary. We have the power to agree or not agree with our enemy, and we have the free will to choose.

I do not want to make light of this choice but sometimes, it's as easy as saying 'no' in the face of temptation and many times, it is not. We win sometimes and fall to the temptation the next time. There are some ways of the world that feel better in the moment than God's ways but we end up paying and sacrificing something in the long run.

Enemy 3

If we have our own will and sinful nature to wrestle with, then so does every other person. Another's sinful nature will be for themselves and not for us. Other people can make decisions to satisfy themselves but this can hurt us. Lies, cons and scams surround us, deceiving us into making decisions that could rob us of anything and everything.

1 Samuel chapter 13 shows how the first king of Israel, King Saul, starts off his reign well as he chooses God's way. Then he begins his slide down the slope of people-pleasing and fulfilling his own desire to be respected. When he oversteps his position as king and offers the burnt offering that only God's appointed priest should perform, he offers up excuses in verses 11–13 that exemplify his fear of rejection Samuel says, "'What have you done?' And Saul said, 'When I saw that the people were scattering, and that you did not come within the days appointed, and that

the Philistines had assembling at Michmash, I said, 'Now the Philistines will come down against me at Gilgal, and I have not sought the favor of the LORD.' So I forced myself and offered a burnt offering.'" He wanted his soldiers and his subjects' approval more than he wanted God's approval. These decisions led to the LORD rejecting Saul as king. And then, David shows up on the scene. Verse 14 of chapter 16 even says, "Now the Spirit of the LORD departed from Saul, and a harmful spirit from the LORD tormented him." King Saul might have been enticed and tormented by the enemy but his sinful nature took the bait. Saul becomes jealous of David, tries to kill David, and hunts David all through the remaining chapters of 1 Samuel. But it's from David's point of view that makes my point about us having a third enemy. David was simply living his life for the LORD and he received opposition, hatred, and several attempts on his life because Saul gave into his own will and sinful nature.

In the four Gospel books, the Jewish chief priests and teachers of God's Law become jealous of Jesus, hunt Jesus, hate Jesus, and plot to kill Jesus. Jesus was sinless and did nothing but what God told Him to do but these men were blind to their own sinful nature.

Training

How can we prepare and train for battle by knowing who our enemies are? There is a fine line of knowing about our enemies without dwelling on them. We simply cannot find this balance without prayer and the Holy Spirit guiding us on what and when is enough. Our enemies cannot be removed if we constantly focus and analyze them. This only causes our enemies and their influence over us to grow.

These sham substitutes must be replaced by the real thing. I've been shown that during my Bible study, I need to focus on what I learn about God in the passage I am reading, not on where I fit in the story or who I relate to. When I facilitate during my Tuesday night Bible study, I make sure we are intentional about what we learned about God. The very last passage we talked about in this chapter was Numbers 13. What did we learn about God in that reading? God wanted His people to have something wonderful and was willing to fight for them to have it. God was upset that His people did not trust Him after all they witnessed Him do for them. The enemy here was fear and the Israelites' own will.

These enemies of ours can create conflicts and prolong battles. The devil has strategies, tactics, and shenanigans to keep us tied in knots and ineffective. We must be aware of his ploys and games to tear us from God and His protection. The devil wants to destroy us, and if he can't destroy us because we are protected in Christ, he will destroy what is around us. If we are able to see through his schemes and our own wills, we can maneuver around this with prayer and keep moving forward.

PRAYER

Heavenly Father, You are our shield and protector. As Jesus taught us to pray, "Lead us not into temptation, but deliver us from evil" (Matthew 6:13). Save us from evil forces and their schemes to separate me from You and cause doubt. Help us recognize their schemes and turn to You. You know more than we do about our enemy, so help us trust Your direction on avoiding evil by following Your commands. Holy Spirit, convict us when our wills are separating from God's will and leading us into disobedience. Remove the scales from our eyes and open our hearts to perceive You and Your conviction. You are our guide and counselor, so strengthen us where we are weak. Convict us of where we think incorrectly about God our Father. Show us where in our hearts and lives we do not trust Him but lean on our own understanding.

CHAPTER 4

EXPOSE ENEMY TACTICS

In the process of writing this book, my printer decided that it was going to mutiny and only print every other line. I work and edit better with a printed page, and I was ready to throw the printer out the window. Does my printer have a brain and decide against me? No. Was my printer inhabited by antagonistic gremlins? It felt that way. But I was furious and felt opposed and vowed I was giving up and quitting this book. Was that my anger being worked up into a froth over something as dumb as an electric printer? Oh, yes. But I was so angry and tired and ready to quit. It wasn't over the printer; it was over one more tiny thing opposing something that I had decided to do. I can't even prove the existence of the resistance, but the timing was ridiculous. What did I do? I couldn't quit because I was past the middle mark. I had to change my plan. I took a break, went to get a snack, drank some water, and reluctantly adapted to working on the computer. And a few days later, with absolutely nothing done on my part, my printer worked as if nothing had happened. I see you, printer.

Whenever something doesn't go my way or go my way easily, I will cry out, "I am being opposed!" However, am I really, and how do I really know? I usually try to look at the result that the opposition is causing. Especially if I am doing something for the Lord. The opposition is there, no matter who is whispering it. We are being heckled, and we are not alone when receiving opposition.

Enemy number one, the devil and evil forces, use the same strategies today that he's been using all along, as written in the Bible. His strategies take away, kill, and destroy anything that matters to God and to us. Why would he do that? Because he is the adversary and opposes whatever might be on your heart, just to bully and be irritating. He has earned those titles that were given to him. He still uses these tricks because they work. If we're almost ready to quit whatever we have set to do or fix, then his wiles still work. Let's expose these tactics used to fight battles against us. Don't be surprised if you recognize these tactics used against you in your battle.

Guerrilla Warfare

I was going to begin this review by giving a list of the ways and strategies humans typically use to fight and win wars. I went to the first battle of the enemy found in Scripture in Genesis 3. This is where the serpent has a conversation with Eve and begins to ask a series of questions that leads to the downfall. Here, I noticed it wasn't the typical confrontational warfare. No, the serpent was sneaky and crafty, using more of a style of guerrilla warfare. Switching my plan, I used a search engine to define guerrilla warfare and the US Department of Justice website gives the following explanation:

> **Annotation:** Guerrilla warfare is part of a subversive effort to overthrow an existing political system; it uses flexibility in a span of coercion that extends from conversation through terrorism and open conventional war.
>
> **Abstract:** Guerrillas are small bands that operate from base areas. Their advantages are knowledge of the population, knowledge of terrorist tactics, mobility, and numerical superiority at a selected point of action. Guerrilla groups focus on the dissatisfactions of a population and use the media as a forum to present ideas, pose questions, and publicize activities. The media also becomes a recruitment tool to expand the number of guerrillas. Since guerrilla forces are relatively small, they must only engage in military confrontations at points and times when they have numerical superiority. They act quickly and then withdraw before enemy reinforcements arrive. Mass, strike, and disperse are strategic elements of successful guerrilla operations. Guerrilla activities include intelligence operations, psychological warfare, sabotage, assassinations, and terrorist acts designed to inject fear and instability in the populace. As a guerrilla group grows in num-

> bers and secures territory, it engages in conventional warfare, followed by consolidation and the establishment of a political organization.[10]

This definition fits exactly the order of how things happened in this passage of Genesis 3. Here are the guerrilla warfare tactics used by our enemy the devil/serpent (either as the website stated or expanded):

Mutiny	leading others to question the leader's decisions
Starts small	just one ______ (fill in the blank)
Small personal attack	hitting opponent where it will cause the most damage
Ally	appear friendly to be involved
Hides	Not out in the open, hides to the point of questioning their existence

The serpent started with just one question. That one question led Eve to question God's commands and decide on her own what was good. The serpent planted the landmine and watched it all explode as the humans walked right over it. Kill and destroy. He killed and destroyed not only the garden, but their relationship with God. Nothing was ever the same.

I experienced this tactic of questioning as I was inter-

10 Beachem, P. "Guerrilla Warfare: Strategies and Tactics." *International Terrorism: The Decade Ahead*, edited by Jane Rae Buckwalter, Office of Justice Programs, U.S. Department of Justice, 1989, pp. 127–132. *NCJRS Virtual Library*, https://www.ojp.gov/ncjrs/virtual-library/abstracts/guerrilla-warfare-strategies-and-tactics-international-terrorism. Accessed 31 July 2024.

ceding for someone else. At first, I thought these were my own thoughts and really doubted that my directions were from the Holy Spirit. I recall questions such as, "Why are you praying for that person? Did the Holy Spirit really tell you to pray about this? That person couldn't care less about you right now, let them lie in their own choices," being thrown my way. I would listen to these questions and alter the wording of my prayers, not to be as bold as before, just in case I was wrong. I would qualify my requests and water them down. I would take up more time complaining and seeking validation that I was doing the right thing, then getting to the business of interceding. It was during a Bible study of Genesis 3 that I realized what side the questions were really coming from. I remember the question the serpent starts off with, "Did God really say...?" It caught my attention, and I thought, wait, I got asked that question! This is the enemy trying to stop me from praying about this!

In the garden, the devil was on his own and did not have a numerous army with him. That wouldn't have worked and would have been way too obvious. Depending on the situation he wants to oppose, is what form of tactics he will use. If he has the advantage or popular opinion, he will switch tactics. Any leader would.

Conventional Warfare

Conventional warfare methods are more common with what we know about war, read in books, and see in war movies. This style is more familiar to us, but no less sneaky when we don't recognize them:

Limited God	"God is unable to _____(fill in the blank)"
Mutiny	Lead others to question the leader's decisions
Doubt God	"Did the Lord really say...?"
Sent by God	"The LORD sent me to destroy you"
Strength	Have more strength and power than opponent
Intimidation	Overwhelm with size, skill, weapons, number
Skills	Better skills than opponent
Maneuvers, Tactics	Use tricks, traps, lead astray
Spies	Gather information about opponent to be used against them
Weapons	Use best, newest technology
Outnumber	Have more soldiers, more weapons, more information, than opponent
Surprise	Use camouflage, hiding, sneak attack
Large Targeted Hit	Hit opponent to cause the most damage
Personal Hit	Attack something opponent cares about more than themselves
Timing	Attack after a victory
No Allies	All alone, no one to save them
Mocking	"Just who are you trusting in?"
History of Wins	Review past victories
Unrelenting Attacks	Repeat unmercifully

Example 1

The above list of the most commonly used battle strategies is the same strategies used by the enemies against Israel and Judah. We will look at several battles from Scripture that illustrate the use of these tactics so we can learn how the enemy uses them. For the conventional warfare style, let's begin with the battle where David meets Goliath found in 1 Samuel chapter 17. We will look for the tactics used against the Israelite army. We will look in more depth at David's response in another chapter.

The first verse tells the positions of both sides. The Philistine forces are gathered on one side of the valley with the Israelites on the other side. Notice that the Philistine enemy army has planted themselves on the land of Judah, the tribe the Messiah will descend from. Interesting choice for the enemy.

Next, we are given the physical traits of a Philistine, who is hailed as their champion, named Goliath. He is a giant and overwhelming in size and strength. He is wearing heavy armor, a bronze helmet, and armor on his legs. His weapons are a bronze javelin, a huge spear, and his own personal shield bearer. Goliath doesn't even have to use them to cause intimidation.

In verses eight through ten, this champion stood and shouted to the ranks of Israel, taunting and challenging them to do something, to prove something, which is mocking and using personal attacks. And yet, Israel did nothing because they were in dismay and terror. This happened every day for forty days, morning and night, in unrelenting attacks.

David appears now, and at this time, he has the Spirit with him as he was already anointed by the judge Samuel earlier in 1 Samuel 16:13. David is not a soldier yet, but a visitor bringing food to his soldier brothers. While there, Goliath comes out for his daily mocking and taunting of not just Israel but their God. Overhearing this speech, David takes offense for God.

As David walks out to meet Goliath, David has disdain, mockery, and curses thrown his way. Verses 43–44, "And the Philistine said to David, 'Am I a dog, that you come to me with sticks?' And the Philistine cursed David by his gods. The Philistine said to David, 'Come to me, and I will give your flesh to the birds of the air and to the beasts of the field!'"

David's response shows that David is very aware of what this battle is about. It's not only about the Philistines versus the Israelites, it's about the defilement of God, His name, and His Promised Land. David replies in verses 45–47:

> You come to me with a sword and with a spear and with a javelin, but I come to you in the name of the Lord of hosts, the God of the armies of Israel, whom you have defiled. This day the Lord will deliver you into my hand, and I will strike you down and cut off your head. And I will give the dead bodies of the host of the Philistines this day to the birds of the air and to the beasts of the earth, that all the earth may

> know that there is a God in Israel, and that all this assembly may know that the Lord saves not with the sword and spear. For the battle is the Lord's, and He will give you into our hand.

David kills Goliath by slinging the one rock on his first try, with no sword or spear. David fulfills his earlier threat by cutting off the head of the champion with the champion's own sword. David, trained in the wilderness and armed by the Spirit when he was anointed king, is able to see the battle for the spiritual conflict that it is. He meets the challenge boldly, and the Philistines, with the champion they trusted in beheaded, turn and run. The attack was thwarted, and the Philistines fled, just as it is written in James 4:7 (NIV), "Resist the devil, and he will flee from you."

Why Fight God?

Then what did the devil gain from inciting this battle? Why does the enemy go up against God ever? In Genesis, he was able to facilitate the destruction of Eden and man's relationship with God. But in this battle, David and the Israelites had a huge victory. From the looks of Goliath and the strength of the Philistine army, paired with the low state of King Saul and how afraid the Israelites were, the Philistines should have won. Even David's showing up wasn't that much of a threat to the enemy. He is looked down on first by his brother and then everyone, trying to get another man's armor on him to make him feel small and insignificant.

The Bible shows but does not tell. There are always several reasons the Lord does what He does, but I am going to choose to focus on King Saul. In chapter 15 of 1 Samuel, King Saul and the Israelites won the battle with the Amalekites before this one with the Philistines. However, he had disobeyed God in collecting the spoils by not destroying everything and keeping what Saul thought was good, including sparing the Amalekite king. This led to the Spirit of the LORD departing from Saul, and harmful spirits began tormenting him as 1 Samuel 16:14 states. The LORD will leave someone in their sin if one consistently chooses to disobey him as Saul did. The prophet Samuel also removes himself from Saul's life as mentor and adviser. So, the devil has already tempted Saul, the very first king of Israel, not to trust God, and their relationship is destroyed. Saul endured forty tormenting days of degrading taunts from the Philistines and did not turn to the LORD for forgiveness or help. If the devil has the king separated from the LORD, then next is taking the Promised Land. The devil attempts this, but God prevails, keeping His Promised Land without King Saul.

Example 2

As the story of God's people continues, David confronts battle after battle as he fights Israel's enemies throughout his reign. His descendants will continue these conflicts as their enemies attempt to destroy both Israel and Judah. However, the tactics used against them are the same.

One of these descendants, King Hezekiah, is threatened by Sennacherib, king of Assyria, in 2 Kings 18. Hezekiah's reign is over 200 years after the reign of King David. The account given says that the Assyrian king seized fortified cities in Judah and then demanded silver and gold from King Hezekiah. Not only did Hezekiah pay this demand, but he also stripped it from the Lord's temple to do so. However, that appeasement only empowered the bully. Instead, the Assyrian king brought the battle to Jerusalem, where King Hezekiah ruled.

The Assyrian Field Commander taunts King Hezekiah and Israel with the following speech in verses 19–25:

> And the Rabshakeh said to them, "Say now to Hezekiah, 'Thus says the great king, the king of Assyria: On what do you rest this trust of yours? Do you think that mere words are strategy and power for war? In whom do you now trust, that you have rebelled against me? Behold, you are trusting now in Egypt, that broken reed of a staff, which will pierce the hand of any man who leans on it. Such is Pharaoh king of Egypt to all who trust in him. But if you say to me, 'We trust in the LORD our God,' is it not he whose high places and altars Hezekiah has removed, saying to Judah and to Jerusalem, 'You shall worship before this altar in Jerusalem'? Come now, make a wager with my master the king of Assyria: I will give you two thousand horses, if you are able on your part to set riders on them. How then can you repulse a single captain among the least of my master's servants, when you trust in Egypt for

> chariots and for horsemen? Moreover, is it without the LORD that I have come up against this place to destroy it? The LORD said to me, 'Go up against this land and destroy it.'

He continues in verses 28–36, speaking directly to the people with this:

> Then the Rabshakeh stood and called out in a loud voice in the language of Judah: "Hear the words of the great king, the king of Assyria! Thus says the king: Do not let Hezekiah deceive you, for he will not be able to deliver you out of my hand. Do not let Hezekiah make you trust in the Lord by saying, 'The Lord will surely deliver us, and this city will not be given into the hand of the king of Assyria.' Do not listen to Hezekiah, for thus says the king of Assyria: Make your peace with me and come out to me. Then each of you will eat of his own vine, and each one of his own fig tree, and each one of you will drink the water of his own cistern, until I come and take you to a land like your own land, a land of grain and wine, a land of bread and vineyards, a land of olive trees and honey, that you may live, and not die. And do not listen to Hezekiah when he misleads you by saying, 'The Lord will deliver us.' Has any one of the gods of the nations ever delivered his land from the hand of the king of Assyria? Where are the gods of Hamath and Arpad? Where are the gods of Sepharvaim, Hena, and Ivvah? Have

they delivered Samaria from my hand? Who among all the gods of the lands have delivered their lands out of my hand, that the Lord should deliver Jerusalem out of my hand?' But the people were silent and answered him not a word, for the king's command was, "Do not answer him."

Using the chart, let's look at this intimidation speech, which has several textbook warfare tactics:

Mocking	v19 Just who are you trusting in?
No allies	v21–22 You can't trust Egypt or the Lord, neither can save you
Sent by God	v25 The Lord sent me to destroy you
Mutiny	v29–30 Do not trust King Hezekiah or the Lord
History of wins	v33–35 Lists past wins where gods did not save

The details are different, but the plotline is the same. Our enemy uses the same tactics to push King Hezekiah around that he used with King Saul. King Hezekiah opens the door for his enemy by paying the demand and not consulting God first. There is the temptation put to Hezekiah to not trust the LORD, but unlike Saul, he turns to the LORD to plead for deliverance in chapter 19. Jerusalem is saved by the angel of the LORD striking the enemy camp, and Sennacherib withdraws to go home.

Example 3

These war tactics, both guerrilla and conventional, can be found throughout the Bible. The devil tries no matter what our relationship with God is. He tries disciples and apostles, as well as those close to God and those far away. He has nothing to lose and will not stop his attempts. We will never reach a level where the devil doesn't tempt us to forsake God. His boldest attempt is in Matthew 4:1–11, where he tempts Jesus. He is using guerrilla tactics, asking questions to tempt Jesus not to trust His Father. His timing is after Jesus was baptized and God Himself confirmed that Jesus was His Son and was pleased. Notice the tactic of timing, after a victory.

The first two tests of the three begin with the enemy taunting, "If you are the Son of God…" There are more effective, quicker ways (in our limited opinion) to do things than God's way. The first temptation is to make bread to feed himself instead of waiting until God provides food. The second is to immediately prove that God will save Jesus instead of waiting for God's timing. The same words, "If you are the Son of God…" are used when Jesus is hanging on the cross. "If you are the Son of God, come down off that cross" (paraphrased from Matthew 27:40). Isn't that the temptation offered to Jesus? To prove Himself and God? He could prove He is good and powerful and mighty, and choose a different way than dying on the cross and then being raised from the dead three days later. Trusting God's way when the physical evidence before us leads to the conclusion that God's way isn't working. Not to do things God's way is a temptation for all of us who try to follow Him.

And remember, the third test is the giving of land, which was reviewed in chapter 2. The land isn't the devil's to give, but he really doesn't stop trying to trick us into believing he has way more power and territory than he really does. The devil even tried to trick tired, hungry, and thirsty Jesus.

Application

What are some of the battles we could face as followers of Christ where we use these tactics? In our ministries, the battle could be for the ministry to succeed and grow. That might include attracting people to help and attracting the people that need the help, getting donations, increasing in numbers, and creating a budget. I have been a part of many Christian businesses that start off with standards about how they run their business and the employees they include. As they grow, they need help, and instead of waiting for the correct person to be sent, they lower the standards. Instead of waiting for the funds to begin a new program, they yoke themselves with an unbeliever or a government as a partner. In our families, the battle might be to have healthy relationships. That might include balancing time between work and family or agreeing to a budget. That might include having to deal with children who are walking away from Jesus Christ and following popular worldly trends. In our prayers, the battle might be to intercede for others. That might include praying for someone who has hurt you or your family, or praying for someone you don't like. This might include discouragement and wrestling with God as our prayers go unanswered or the situation gets worse.

These situations and countless others can make us want to push away from God's way of doing things because they don't bring about immediate results. During a training session for teachers, the point was made that yelling and extreme punishment would get immediate results to stop the students' undesirable behavior. However, even though the student's behavior changed at that moment, the motive behind the behavior was not addressed, and the behavior would repeat. Using these strategies can get us what we want for the moment, but what if what we want isn't good for us and drives us further from the Lord?

Our enemies will use whatever means necessary to accomplish their goals. They will justify the means they use to reach what they want. The strategies they deploy have become common practice used by the world. We should review if these strategies are the way God wants us to fight for Him. These are effective tactics that can win the battle, but what are we "winning" if we do not follow Christ and become more like Him? Are we winning more souls for Christ or getting better numbers? I think there is a very real danger of using these worldly tactics to get what we want with no regard to the effect on the soul. We must check our hearts and motives on how we act during our battles, or we will leave God's way behind us.

Let's look at the way we might use the world's tactics as we are fighting:

Limited God	"God is unable or unwilling, so I must do for myself"
Mutiny	"God told me something different"
Doubt God	"Did the Lord really say...?"
Sent by God	"The LORD sent me to tell you"
Strength	I must do something by willpower or discipline alone
Intimidation	Gloat and flaunt skills, connections, information
Skills	Argue and debate better than opponent
Maneuvers, Tactics	Manipulate by lying, withdrawing, nagging
Spies	Ask others for information or advice first, gossip
Weapons	Twist a verse to prove our point
Outnumber	Have more people praying, more information, getting to other people before the other person can
Surprise	Surprise confrontations, rapid-fire questions
Large Targeted Hit	Hitting opponent where it will cause the most damage
Personal Hit	Knowing and throwing past sins or weaknesses back during arguments
Timing	Knowing when to hit for most effect
No Allies	Using words such as normal, majority, everyone else
Mocking	Using words such as stupid, illogical, fool
History of Wins	Lists past wins when tactics worked
Unrelenting Attacks	Unmercifully repeated until the person is worn down and gives in

We could be using these tactics unknowingly. These are the way things have always been done, and we don't give a thought before doing them. However, God cares deeply for the motives and condition of our hearts.

What do we do? How do we avoid using these tactics? First, we pray for conviction of our methods and direction on what to do about them. Every situation is different, but we aren't working with formulas here. Our God is not a robot or a machine, and neither are we, as we are made in His image.

Some of these can be dealt with by exercising self-control over our mouths. Mic-drops and putting people in their place included. We love to fix things and save people. The number of times I have thought "I know I could just fix them and the entire situation if I could just tell them about themselves, LORD!!!" I always get a "No." However, I do believe the Lord does sometimes give us a verse or a passage for someone, but there are some guidelines I have learned before I tell someone.

Before we speak, here are some clarifying questions we could ask ourselves. One, is it encouraging or is it a conviction? Before we offer a judgment, we must remove the plank out of our own eye and apply it to ourselves first. Two, if I determine it is a judgment or conviction, I ask the Holy Spirit to open their own eyes about it. Three, even if it is an encouragement, I ask the Holy Spirit to provide the perfect setting and a strong nudge before I offer. Or even better, they ask me. Otherwise, the mouth remains closed. If you are unable, involve the Holy Spirit to shut it for you. I promise He will. I have applied all of these and the Holy Spirit has done every one for me.

Some of these tactics fall under our distrust of God, Jesus, and the Holy Spirit. Some of these strategies are how we want our own way immediately, and we will do what we must to have it. These two go hand in hand. Our will does not align with what we suspect God's will is, so we twist, manipulate, lie, cheat, nag, and intimidate. Twisting a verse out of context to get what we want is a tactic the devil uses.

Being angry with others and calling someone a fool, including synonyms such as stupid or idiot, is a sin, as Jesus states in Matthew 5:22. Degrading someone over any difference they have from us is a sin, as it says in Romans 2:1–3. Gossip is slander and is included in the list of wickedness in Romans 1:29. I mention these because I know that, for me, finding out that I was offending God by my lack of trust and pride, that I was sinning and being wicked, was discomfiting. I was flustered and humbled when convicted that I was racking up sins unknowingly.

Beyond just sinning, I was recently convicted of my motive for asking others to join me in prayer for the outcome I wanted for the person I was praying for. Jesus does tell us in Matthew 18:20, "For where two or three are gathered in my name, there am I among them." Maybe if my friend who is really good at praying and my other friend who is close to the Lord were praying, then something for the better will happen. For my situation in that circumstance, the Holy Spirit revealed that I held the belief in my heart that it wasn't enough for just me to ask and that I needed others for the prayer to be answered. Do we ask others to pray because the greater the number that are asking, the better chance we have for an agreement? I have learned the lesson to listen when God told me to pray by myself in the closet, and the lesson to wait before I invite others to pray. Each situation could be different depending on what God is doing in our lives.

Training

How can we prepare and train for battles by learning our enemy's tactics?

The devil and all his company know the Bible and know human nature. They learn and use this knowledge against us to try to separate us from God and His Kingdom. He has schemes and tricks that continue to work on us. But noticing the trick and the trap will keep us from falling for it, help us to respond better, and keep us focused toward our goal. We will not outsmart or out-maneuver our enemies, so we must be aware of not just the enemies' shenanigans, but know for ourselves what the real thing would be.

Studying the Bible is part of our preparation and training. Reading and listening to lectures is the least effective way to learn, so we engage in Bible study on our own and with a group. Iron sharpens the iron of the sword of Truth, which is the Word of God. There are so many excellent Bible studies available to us. Find one. Use one.

Start one. We are not expected to know it all, but we must start somewhere.

Checking with the Holy Spirit about our heart and motives can become part of our prayers. We will be held responsible for how we go about spreading the gospel and shining His light. The end result does not justify the means. If the Holy Spirit says it's acceptable, let's do it. Preparation and training takes prayer with God, communion with Jesus, study of His Word, and leaning on the Holy Spirit for insight. What is more important to you—winning the battle or obeying God? We need to decide how we think God will answer that.

PRAYER

Lord God Almighty, You and only You are worthy of our worship. Forgive us of our sins and lead us not into temptation. Forgive us for insisting that our ways are better than yours, that our ways get results. Give us discernment and insight to see through the enemy's tactics and guide us on how we should respond. Help us to decipher if we should be on guard against our enemies, our own nature wanting its way, or just life here on this alien planet. Bring our focus on You and what You would have us learn and do for Your kingdom. We want to draw closer to You, but we aren't sure how. We need Your assistance to not fear our enemy but to have reverence for You, our Almighty God, the One True God, worthy of all creation's worship.

CHAPTER 5

IDENTIFY THE BATTLE

I was praying for one of my youth group students who had just received a rejection. She was going off to college and had applied for a club she really wanted to join. She had not been accepted, and she was upset as this would have helped her progress in her major. I was praying about her and asking what the lesson was in her not being accepted. I perceived an answer to my prayers, that the Lord was guarding her spiritually by not allowing her to be accepted physically. And from that, I began to see this overlap of physical and spiritual in many situations. I began to work out the spreadsheet below to represent what I was beginning to sense.

These three realms, or kingdoms or levels, overlap each other and take place at the same time now in the present. This is not a new concept, but I think we forget that the realms affect each other when dealing with our lives. The physical realm is this tangible earth and all that it holds. We, as limited, material creations, are limited to this physical world on this physical earth. We can use our five senses to prove all of this physical world's tangible existence. Of the three members of the Trinity, I feel Jesus represents the physical realm, as He came into the physical world as a human. The spiritual realm occupies the same space and present time as Earth but has the addition of heaven. However, the spiritual is just beyond our five physical senses to capture. We might perceive this realm, but it is not obvious or substantial. These two interact and have an impact on each other. What happens in the spiritual world can play out on the stage of the physical world. What happens in the physical world can impact the spiritual world. What happens in the present time in the physical and spiritual realms will affect the eternal kingdom. The eternal kingdom will take place in an age to come, in a new heaven and earth, beyond anything we can imagine and beyond a timeframe we can imagine.

	Realm/ Kingdom	Our Interaction	Time Frame	World Placement	Trinity
1	Eternal	beyond our imagination	future	new heaven	God
2	Spiritual	perceive beyond senses	present	heaven and earth	Holy Spirit
3	Physical	5 senses used	present	earth	Jesus Christ

We can take what we know about the different realms and apply it to the other realms. This will improve our understanding as we learn more about the Trinity and the kingdom of heaven. Jesus used this method of teaching, using the known to explain the unknown. He gave spiritual lessons by telling parables, using an illustration they would all know to draw parallels with a kingdom they were confused about. If Jesus uses the physical realm to help us understand the spiritual realm, then they must be very similar and parallel each other.

Our trials and tribulations seem as if they are only about the physical kingdom, but the real fight is over the spiritual kingdom with eternal implications. If Paul discusses in Ephesians 6 that we do not fight against flesh and blood, then we are not fighting over flesh and blood either. We have an enemy that uses this against us, spins the narrative so we are fighting the wrong battle on the wrong front. What a diversion, what a decoy, what a trick to make it seem like it's over a toothbrush, when it's really over saving someone's soul from eternal hell. What a disguise to lead us to believe it's just a play and not that serious, when it's the most serious fight we will be involved in.

Old Testament Example

There is a war over the Israelites leaving Egypt found in the book of Exodus. The surface fight seems that it's a power struggle between the Israelites and the Egyptians. The Israelites are given the opportunity to leave their physical oppression and slavery of 400 years. But on the spiritual level, there is a battle happening over worship, spiritual oppression, and slavery to the enemy and the little gods. In Exodus 3 (NIV), God appears to Moses and, through the course of their conversation, God mentions the subject of worship several times. In verse 12, God says to Moses, "I will be with you. And this will be the sign to you that it is I who have sent you: When you have brought the people out of Egypt, you will worship God on this mountain." And also in verse 18, when God is explaining to Moses what he will say to the Israelite elders, "... Then you and the elders are to go to the king of Egypt and say to him, 'The Lord, the God of the Hebrews, has met with us. Let us take a three-day journey into the wilderness to offer sacrifices to the Lord our God.'" In Exodus 5:1 (NIV), Moses and Aaron go to Pharaoh and say, "This is what the Lord, the God of Israel, says: 'Let my people go, so that they may hold a festival to me in the wilderness.'" Moses and Aaron repeat the same ultimatum to Pharaoh as a warning before seven of the ten plagues. This is a battle over who the Israelites worship.

Usually, we always quote the first part of Moses' well-known statement, "Let My people go," but leave out the second part, "so that they may serve me." That would be for the people of God to serve only God. They are not to serve Pharaoh or any of those lesser gods. Pharaoh wanted the Israelites to serve him by keeping them bound and enslaved to him, in chains and a prison. Like cults, where choices aren't offered, the leader is worshiped without question, and the followers do all the leader says. God wanted the Israelites to serve Him by setting them free and giving them their own land where they could choose to follow Him or not.

The plagues were not just random displays of God's power. On the physical surface, the nature of each plague just appears to be an interesting choice. However, the plagues were battles over worship in the spiritual realms. Each plague confronts and overpowers at least one Egyptian god. The following list is paraphrased from a *Zondervan Academic* blog, "What the Bible Tells Us About the 10 Plagues of Egypt," and gives what Egyptian god the plague was aimed towards.

The first plague, turning the Nile into blood, was for the god of the Nile, the goddess of the Nile, and a guardian of the Nile.

The second plague, the uncountable frogs, was for the goddess of birth who had a frog head.

The third plague, the overwhelming gnats, was for the god of the desert storms.

The fourth plague, the overwhelming flies, was for the sun god and another god possibly represented by the fly.

The fifth plague, the death of livestock, was for the goddess with a cow head and the bull god, symbols of fertility.

The sixth plague, boils, was for the goddess with power over disease, the pestilence god and the healing goddess.

The seventh plague, hail, was for the sky goddess, the god of crops and fertility and the god of desert storms.

The eighth plague, locusts, was for the sky goddess and the god of crops and fertility.

The ninth plague, darkness, was for the sun gods and the sky goddesses.

The tenth plague, death of the firstborn sons, was for the god of reproduction, the goddess who was at childbirth, the goddess who protected children and Pharaoh's firstborn son, who was considered a god.[11]

The fight on the physical level is for freedom of God's chosen people from slavery and oppression from a world power. The fight on the spiritual level taking place at the same time and place is for the freedom of God's people from spiritual slavery and oppression by false gods and the devil. God displayed His might and trustworthiness in showdown after showdown as the devil fought back for the territory he had ruled for 400 years. God was faithful to His promise to Abraham, who wasn't even physically alive to witness it. The worship of God and only God will bring our biggest battles. God wants us to sincerely love and worship only Him. The temptation not to love and worship Him will bring evil to test, divide, and conquer.

New Testament Examples

To further illustrate the three realms taking place at the same present time, I'll review a passage in the Gospel of Mark. There are four stories that happen in rapid succession in Mark 4:35 through 5:43 (NIV). This section begins with the disciples in a boat while Jesus sleeps

11 Schnittjer, Gary Edward. *What the Bible Tells Us About the 10 Plagues of Egypt*. Zondervan Academic, 2 May 2018, https://zondervanacademic.com/blog/what-the-bible-tells-us-about-the-10-plagues-of-egypt. Accessed 26 Apr. 2024.

through a storm. Then they encounter a demon-possessed man, and Jesus casts the demons into pigs, then the synagogue leader begs Jesus to come heal his dying daughter, which is interrupted by the woman bleeding for twelve years touching Jesus's outer garment. Although lengthy, I will go over each because they each represent a portion of our lives that we struggle with, and how this three-in-one theory can be applied.

Jesus Calms the Storm

Verses 35–41 of chapter four begin with Jesus suggesting that they take the boat they are sitting in and cross over the sea to the other side. Verse 37 describes a furious squall rising up and waves breaking over the boat, filling it up with water. Jesus, however, is in the stern, the back of the boat where the driver sits, but he's asleep on a pillow. The disciples awaken and question Jesus whether He cares that they are dying. He arises, rebuking the wind and calming the sea with a command of "Peace! Be still!" before He addresses them in verse 40. "He said to them, "Why are you so afraid? Have you still no faith?"

I want to point out some details here for background knowledge. At the beginning of chapter 4, Jesus is already in a boat teaching the people on the shore. Verse 35 tells us evening had fallen, so this part happened in the dark night. This could be why experienced fishermen were caught off guard by this storm and possibly went in a boat as they were unprepared for a trip. *Thayer's Greek Lexicon* defines the word "squall" as a whirlwind—a storm breaking forth from black thunderclouds in furious gusts, with floods of rain, and throwing everything topsy-turvy, not just a steadily blowing wind. This was a frightening storm.

On the surface, what we can see is the fight to stay alive and afloat when the weather wants to stop them. The wind was doing its best to drown the boat with them inside. None of them could fix this situation, so they finally turn to Jesus and then accuse Him of not caring whether or not they physically perish. Jesus woke up and rebuked the wind, which is playing the part of the adversary here. Notice there is no mention of the devil being the source of this storm, but the weather is acting the part. Jesus commands the sea to be at peace and be still, and the sea responds immediately with great calm, not even the slightest waves. And turning to His disciples, what does Jesus address? Their faith. Their spiritual faith. The fear that replaced their trust. The fear that turned them timid and cowardly, replacing their confidence in His character. Does He care whether we physically perish? Yes, He does, as we will see in chapter 5 of Mark when He restores the synagogue leader's daughter. However, His biggest concern is their spiritual health. This tribulation is their training. Jesus knows what these men are going to face in the future, and they need to know without any doubts, who Jesus is and who answers to Him. Because of this storm, they witness His glory and His reign over the wind and the waves. And now so do we.

Jesus Heals a Possessed Man

Jesus, the disciples, and the boats make it to the other side in chapter 5. Jesus barely makes it out of the boat when He is confronted by a man with an unclean spirit. We are told in the next few verses that this man lives among the tombs and no one could bind him with chains or shackles, or he would break them. Verses 6–7 says the possessed man recognizes Jesus from afar, runs up and bows down before Him, and then begins crying out questions in a loud voice. Jesus directs in verse 8 (NIV), "Come out of this man, you impure spirit!" This command is followed by a conversation about how many spirits there actually are taking up residence. The leader of the evil spirits begs Jesus not to send them out of the region, but requests to be sent into the herd of swine nearby instead. Jesus gives permission, and off they go into the pigs, and the pigs then run violently down the steep bank to drown in the sea.

Here is additional information that I'll just leave right here. Pigs can swim. I did not know this until a friend and I were discussing this passage, and she told me. I looked it up to verify, and pigs can instinctively swim, which means that the evil spirits drowned the herd of pigs.

The fight on the physical surface is that this unpredictable, possessed man might hurt Jesus and his disciples. If he were too strong to be shackled or chained up, imagine what he could do to a person. From the outside, the man looked crazy and disturbed. This man is not bound physically, but bound spiritually because of the unclean spirit residing in his body. This man resides among the dead, among the buried bones. The unclean spirits cause the man to cut himself, slowly destroying him. The evil spirits have isolated him, physically and spiritually, and this man is beyond hope. All these unclean spirits know is torment as they torment this man unmercifully and then accuse Jesus of tormenting them. The spirits accuse Jesus of tormenting them, which is just pure projection on their part. We judge others by what we are ourselves. There is no one to seek Jesus on this man's behalf. However, Jesus knew and went across the sea to save this one man because this whole trip was at Jesus' request in Mark 4:35 (NIV), "Let us go over to the other side." This spiritual battle was about saving one man for eternity, and he was not even Jewish. The disciples were able to witness evil bow down to Jesus and do what He commanded. He crossed all that way to save that man not only physically, but spiritually and eternally.

That man was the only one saved that day, as the reactions from the owners of the pigs and the people of that region were to push Jesus away and out. Jesus and the disciples had to cross back over the water. Once back on land, they were surrounded quickly by another crowd. In Mark 5:22, we are introduced to Jairus, one of the synagogue officials. Jairus sees Jesus and falls at His feet. Jairus begs Jesus to please come back home with him, so Jesus can lay hands on Jairus' dying daughter so that she will be made well again. Jesus agrees and goes with Jairus.

However, the story of one daughter gets interrupted by another daughter's story.

Jesus Heals The Woman with Blood

In verses 25 and 26, we are told details about a woman who had blood flow for twelve years, which no physician or amount of money could heal. But she heard about Jesus and was determined to just touch His garment, for she knew if she could just do that, she would be healed. Verse 29 says she was cured instantly. Jesus then immediately sensed that power had gone out of Him, turned to the crowd, crushing up against Him, and wanted to know who had touched Him. The disciples, in a moment of unguarded what I would term "sass," reply to Him, "You see the crowd pressing around you, and yet you say, 'Who touched me?'" (Mark 5:31). Jesus continued looking for the source. When He finds her, she falls at His feet and tells Him the whole truth. He calls her "Daughter."

Here are some background details concerning this woman. According to Jewish law given in Leviticus 15:25–30, she would have been considered unclean for as long as she had the discharge beyond her monthly period. Her condition would have made her unclean both physically and spiritually. She would not be able to be in public lest she touch anyone else and make them unclean, too. So, no social gatherings such as weddings or funerals, no going to the temple or festivals, no going to the market. For twelve years. She is physically and spiritually imprisoned by her condition.

On the physical surface, the fight seems to be against an incurable disease. No human or amount of money could fix her problem. So she snuck up on Jesus to physically touch just the garment He was wearing so she could be physically healed. According to the law given in Leviticus 15:28–30 (NIV), if the discharge had stopped, she would take two doves or pigeons to the priest for him to make sacrifices to make atonement for her uncleanness in the sight of God. On the spiritual level, this battle was for this woman to get through all the opposition to touch Jesus, who would be the sacrifice, so He could bring atonement and free her from the spiritual oppression of her disorder. With all the people crowding around and brushing up against Him, her touch was different. In Mark 5:30 (NIV) states, "At once Jesus realized that power had gone out from him. He turned around in the crowd and asked, 'Who touched my clothes?'" Among all those who were physically touching Him, Jesus was talking about a different level of touch than a mere physical touch. He wanted whoever touched Him on a spiritual level that brought the healing power from Him to be known. Once she confesses in verse 33, He says to her, "Daughter, your faith has healed you. Go in peace and be freed from your suffering" (Mark 5:34, NIV). Her touch was different from all the other touches because of her trust and faith in Him, and this brought both physical and spiritual healing.

Jesus Restores a Daughter's Life

Meanwhile, Jairus has been standing by while Jesus took the time to heal this woman. While Jesus is telling this woman her faith made her well, some men from Jairus' household came to tell Jairus not to both-er the Teacher because the daughter had died. Jesus ignores their conclusion and tells Jairus directly, "Don't be afraid; just believe" (Mark 5:36, NIV). Jesus continues to Jairus' home, taking only three disciples with Him, and finds a commotion of people crying and wailing loudly. He tells them in verse 39, "Why all this commotion and wailing? The child is not dead but asleep." They laugh at Him and get put outside. Taking the father, the mother, and His three disciples, they all go in with the child. Jesus takes the child's hand and says in Aramaic, "Little girl, arise!" (Mark 5:41). She immediately stands up and walks around. In verse 43, He tells them not to let anyone know about this and to give her something to eat.

Here is some background information. Mourners were important, and I found in my research that there were professional mourners back then. Their job was to wail and weep when someone died. A commotion at a death was the custom, and it was disrespectful and disgraceful if wailing and weeping did not take place. I'm not sure if these mourners even knew the little girl because one second, they are weeping, and the next, they are laughing. The mourners were the skeptics, and they were removed from witnessing the miracle.

The struggle on the physical level is the physical health of a child, a young, beloved daughter. No human could fix this condition, and Jesus is sought out to heal her. But before Jesus can get to the little girl, she dies. The struggle is that the child can no longer be healed or saved, and Jesus is too late. If He could have been there and touched her, she could have been saved from physical death. No point in bothering Jesus now. There is another battle over trusting Jesus when He insists on continuing and says, "Don't be afraid; just believe" (Mark 5:36, NIV). According to *Thayer's Greek Lexicon*, the definition of the Greek word for "afraid" used here is "to be seized with alarm." The very same word is used for the woman with the issue of blood when she is found out by Jesus for touching His fringe. But Jesus just uses the word *believe* when talking with Jairus. What should Jairus believe in exactly? What Jesus can do or who He is? The news that the little girl had died did not stop Jesus from encouraging Jairus or continuing on to his house. This was before Jesus was crucified and resurrected, defeating the power that death had in this physical realm. He was showing that death answered to Him, He did not answer to death. Again, physical death is not the end, unless it is also a spiritual death. And in just a little while, He would fight death and defeat it for us all.

Our Questions Reveal Our Trust

Look at all the accusations Jesus endured over the few days that happened in this passage of Mark we just reviewed:

- From the disciples when they met an unexpected whirlwind—Don't You care whether we perish?
- From the demons, when they encounter Jesus—Are You here to torment me?

- From the people in the area of the pigs—You've taken away my prized possession, and You are not welcome here.
- From the men of Jairus' household—You are too late, and it is beyond restoration.
- From the disciples about touch—What are you talking about?...You're asking "Who touched me?' Dozens have touched You!

What is the real battle here, the underlying question? It is whether God is good and can be trusted. These four situations can be lumped together into situations beyond our control and our own help. Weather and death played adversaries beyond the people's control. Physical and mental health played adversaries beyond the people's ability to receive any human help.

If Jesus heals and speaks with all three levels in mind, then we can deal with our trials and tribulations, our problems and anxieties on all three levels. God uses the physical realm to polish us spiritually to prepare us for eternity. We are the ones falling for the schemes to make the fight seem like it's about anything other than God. This is our chance to pray to God for this insight. Not to ask for our problems to be solved and circumstances changed, but to improve our relationship with God and trust Him for who He is.

Have you ever questioned Jesus if He cared about your life? I know I have, and recently. Have you asked Him if He is here to torment? Maybe you've accused Him of taking what you loved, and you don't want Him around. We have probably told Him He's too late and to never mind, it's beyond His help. That's another thing I have said to Him. Have you wondered what's the difference that faith makes? These are the questions and statements about what we see, hear, feel, and experience. I think we are really asking Jesus if we can trust Him with our physical and spiritual needs and wants. Can we trust Him to care, to assist, to counsel, to encourage, to advise, to help us have faith that makes a difference? Because how can we worship what we don't trust?

Training

How can we prepare and train by identifying what the battle is really about?

Spending all your prayers, energy, and resources on the wrong problem is frustrating and discouraging. That would be fighting on the wrong front. If we don't know where the opposition is coming from, we will send our resources to all possibilities, leaving us depleted with the resources weak and misspent. That would be fighting on all fronts. Knowing what front the fight is on, we can use our prayers and our thoughts on addressing the real struggle.

There is possibly more than one battle, but maybe they are similar. Ask the Holy Spirit for guidance and discernment if the battles are similar or if there are similarities, or which to fight first. Maybe one battle caused the other.

Ask. We are losing our focus and heart with anxiety, fear, and anger.

I have struggled with prayer during different phases throughout my life. The struggle to pray looked like the problem. So, I would read books on how to pray, what to pray, and what prayers work, and what you shouldn't do. Those books and articles all helped, until I went to actually pray. I limped along, blaming myself, until I was shown that my struggle to pray was really from my belief that prayer didn't work. I viewed God as a vending machine, and when my prayers were not answered as I so thoughtfully asked, my trust in prayer and in God crumbled at the 'no.' My trust and faith in God should not be built on if I get my requests just as I ask. That gives me power and puts God within a limit. God is the reward. Talking with Him and discussing possibilities is a gift. My real battle was about how I viewed prayer, not whether I was praying right. Wrong front. And all I had to do was ask for help.

Discovering that the physical and spiritual realms interact and affect each other can help us with our prayers, with our battles, with our trust and faith in God. This view could help us see our struggles and brawls from God's perspective. Our prayers could change, and how we interact with God when we pray will change. This will change how we fight. He loves each of us, and His biggest concern is if we will spend eternity with Him.

PRAYER

Dear Adonai,

You are omnipotent and omniscient. Open our eyes and perception to what You decide is enough for us to know and help us to trust You in that boundary. May we worship You and seek You more in our battles. Give us creativity in our prayers and discussions with You over what we think we see versus the fights we don't see. Give us ideas on how to dream and pray for the impossible and then believe You and Your Word. Strengthen and encourage us to be honest and reverent in our questions about our circumstances. Redirect us when we are fighting about the wrong issue, with all our energy on the wrong front. Thank you for Your presence, Lord.

CHAPTER 6

PREPARING FOR BATTLE

There have been only a few battles in my life that I have been ready for, and that was because someone warned and prepared me. When I decided that I was going to raise money to move and work in Africa, the organization I went with provided great training by telling us what opposition and discouragements to expect while we fundraised. They had been through this many times, noticed the patterns and tactics used, and helped us as we went through them. Things such as how long it would take to raise the money, doing many events with little results, and the type of people and questions that might be at your events. They even went over what could happen once we relocated and direction for how to handle disagreements among teams. When these things happened, I knew how to handle things and what to pray over. There were surprise and sneak attacks, but we could work through them because we were not worn out from fighting all the other things, too.

So first, as followers of Jesus Christ, let's be aware that we will not be able to live in this physical kingdom without skirmishes, conflicts, and battles. We can get better prepared as we learn more about the patterns and typical plays that happen as we encroach on an occupied territory.

God warns His children before they are to be involved in conflicts. We make the conflict even messier by not noticing His warnings or not realizing that we are stepping onto a battleground when we begin prayer or a ministry. But we are not called to prepare in our own strength and with our own methods. There are many instances throughout the Bible that show this preparation by God. I will review the example in the book of Exodus about the Israelites leaving Egypt. God made both Moses and the nation of Israel ready for the huge battle that would take place in order for them to leave Egypt and enter the land God promised.

Preparation of Moses

God begins the evacuation of the Hebrew nation by preparing the one who will lead the Israelites out of Egypt. Chapters 1 and 2 of Exodus narrate how Moses is saved from death and raised by the daughter of the very pharaoh who was trying to kill all male Hebrew babies. In Pharaoh's household, Moses receives physical preparation by education and training in leadership from a world power. Yet, he still empathizes with his own people and is incited to change their harsh treatment when he kills the Egyptian who was beating a fellow Hebrew. Here, his emotions are prepared to love and defend his people. Once Pharaoh seeks his life, Moses runs to the desert, where he is both physically trained to live in the desert and lead a flock, and is spiritually prepared by God through Jethro, the priest of Midian.

Exodus 3 reveals how Moses encounters God in the desert, and they begin their friendship. God divulges to Moses that the Israelites have been crying out to Him about their treatment in Egypt, and He is answering His people's prayers. God sends Moses back into Egypt to notify and prepare the Israelite Elders of the removal plan as well as begin the battle with Pharaoh. The fight that was coming was unfathomable; none of them could have dreamed the spiritual conflict that was raging to keep God's chosen people right there in Egypt, where they were dominated by pagan rule, oppressed and enslaved by lesser gods of the enemy. A massive spiritual battle is about to spill over into the physical realm in Egypt as the entire Israelite family leaves their enslavement.

Preparation of Israel

When Pharaoh uses a power maneuver by multiplying the physical work of the Israelites in Exodus 5, the Hebrew nation is unprepared for such a tactic. In Exodus 5:21, the Hebrew officers come from a meeting with Pharaoh and blame Moses and Aaron for making them odious in Pharaoh's eyes. Trying to appease our enemy is often a strategy we try, hoping that consent will mollify the bully. The devil gained ground here as the Hebrew nation became irate with Moses and God, not their oppressor. The Israelites simply did not know about their enemy and his tactics, nor did they know God and trust Him. The devil is able to turn God's people away from God almost immediately. Even today, we must be ready and vigilant for this tactic.

Often, I wonder why they get mad, as Scripture does not tell us exactly, but this is our typical human behavior: to blame God instead of trusting Him. I know I would be mad if I expected this was going to be easy since God was here and deliverance was so close. In fact, I do get mad when things I expected to go easily or should go easy do not. Help had arrived after years, decades, even centuries of unanswered prayers. God had said He was going to remove them from these circumstances, and now, the situation continues to get worse. God continued His plan even without their confidence.

In the chapters leading up to the final confrontation before Pharaoh lets the Israelites leave, we are able to detect how the Israelites were being mentally and spiritually prepared before the tenth and final plague. The plagues started as well as the on-the-job spiritual training for trusting and believing in their God. As mentioned in a previous chapter, each plague confronted an Egyptian god. These ten plagues are a physical display of the spiritual war about who is the One and Only God.

The first and second plagues were duplicated by Pharaoh's magicians, but by the third plague, the magicians were unable to replicate. Although personally, I find it very strange that the magicians would want to duplicate more blood in their river and conjure up any more frogs just to prove they could. That is our enemy. Our enemy can replicate only so much before he is eclipsed in the contest. Very soon after the beginning of the plagues, it is undeniable who is the Almighty LORD.

Before Moses returned to Egypt from the desert, God gave both warning and preparation in Exodus 4:21–23 that He would take the firstborn son if Pharaoh did not set God's sons free. The tenth plague is the pinnacle of this showdown. By this final plague, in which the first-born sons of the Egyptians died, the Israelites were prepared to do what was required of them. They knew the Lord better now, and all He said was coming to pass. If the Israelites followed the directions given by God, they would be marked for the Lord to pass over them as He moved through Egypt for the tenth plague.

The Nation of Israel had work to do and items to prepare in order to be ready for an epic war they would witness only a portion of with their physical eyes. As laid out in Exodus 12, the blood of a chosen sacrificial lamb must be applied to their door frames, or the firstborn son of that house would die instead. Neighbors in their community must be checked on to make sure they are included and covered by the blood, too. Instructions were to roast this sacrificial lamb and eat it with belt buckled, sandals on feet, staff in hand, and eat in a hurry, ready to go. Get mentally prepared to leave by putting on their traveling clothes. Get physically ready by eating for strength and marking their homes. Get spiritually ready by putting the lamb's blood on the frame of the door. Follow the directions given. Step by step. As they went into the desert, follow the directions given and walk step by step. As they went across the dry ground of the Red Sea floor, follow the directions and walk step by step. It's when they distrusted their God and stopped following, leaning on their own understanding, that they lost their battle to enter the Promised Land. Spoiler alert from Numbers chapters 13 and 14: not one of this generation entered the Promised Land.

Mind, Body, Heart & Spirit

Soldiers ready themselves before they step into battle. They may not know what they will encounter exactly, but they know it will be combat. Their bodies, minds, and emotions are evaluated before they engage in the conflict. Part of this preparation is education, training, and discipline. Think about the physical condition any soldier must be in to endure combat. Their mental condition includes training to mentally handle the stress, fear, and uncertainty of battle. Their emotional condition has to include friendships with fellow soldiers, support from family and friends, and support from health professionals. If soldiers find themselves outside of healthy bodies, healthy minds, or healthy support systems, their ability to persevere and withstand warfare becomes a hindrance, and they could be held back from engaging. Being unhealthy in any of those three areas while fighting in a war could cost lives beyond the soldiers and damage much more than themselves.

The health of our minds, bodies, and emotions must be tested for weak spots and possible places where the enemy can gain ground spiritually. In *The Christian Warfare*, author Dr. D. Martyn Lloyd-Jones discusses how the body, mind, and spirit are interrelated and react with one another. Separating or misdiagnosing between the three can cause great harm.[12] We have work to do to prepare ourselves to fight for our Lord's work. Physical, mental, emotional, and spiritual preparation is work that no one can do for you. It's not too late to get prepared, as your battle is already ongoing.

Health of Mind & Heart

Due to our sinful nature, emotions cannot be considered truth. We are made to feel emotions, but when they get out of control and become extreme, this is a signal that something else is going on in the mind or in the body. The enemy will use our emotions as catalysts and lead us to think they are more reliable than facts. This is a dangerous trap, and we should be aware of misdiagnosing our emotions. Our thoughts lead to emotions, and our thoughts must be taken captive and made obedient to Jesus Christ, as Paul warns us in 2 Corinthians 10:5 (NIV), "We demolish arguments and every pretension that sets itself up against the knowledge of God, and we take captive every thought to make it obedient to Christ."

12 Lloyd-Jones, D. Martyn. *The Christian Warfare: An Exposition of Ephesians 6:10–13*. Baker Publishing Group, 1998.

When our ministry or the outcome of our prayers go off the path we envisioned or expected, we feel disappointment, discouragement, anger, and sorrow. Even when our emotions have merit and are justified, they can drive a wedge between us and God. They have to be monitored and addressed before they move us into trouble. I've known people who completely walked away from God due to their disappointment, as I am sure you have, too. Giving up in lieu of staying and wrestling with God over your expectations and distress can be so tempting when you hurt.

When I find myself in this place of dismay, as I have numerous times, I will free-write about what I expected to happen. I am always shocked at the twisted thinking that bubbles to the surface. For instance, I would be prompted to pray specifically for this person, and then days later, information would come to me that went in the opposite direction of what I prayed about. To be honest, I was not praying consistently, and I blamed my erratic praying on this cycle of praying and getting the opposite answer. I would be hurt, disappointed, and ready to quit praying. Exactly what the enemy wants. I decided to free-write to discover what I was struggling with exactly. I realized a wholehearted expectation that because the Holy Spirit had nudged me to pray specifically, the answer should be as I had prayed that time, and the battle won and the person saved. After all, I was praying for what I was told. I would then take what I had written and physically hold it out before God during my prayer time, taking inspiration from

King Hezekiah in 2 Kings 19:14 when he spread out the enemy's letter before the Lord. Then I waited and listened for an answer to my struggle. Each time, the Holy Spirit would open my eyes to a belief about God that needed to be corrected.

I love the saying, "Expectations are the root of all heartache." Expectations have a way of sneaking up on us, twisting and turning us away from God in the process. Honest communication with Him about all you are feeling, including all the "I thought You would…" has to be done. In the story *The Horse and His Boy* by C.S. Lewis, one of my favorite parts is when Aslan tells the little boy, "Tell me your sorrows."[13] Tell Him your expectations. Tell Him your sorrows. Confess and remove the heartaches to the One who loves you the most.

Health of Body

We are wonderfully as well as intricately made by God. Addressing the health of our physical bodies is as complicated as our bodies are made. There are so many opinions and beliefs concerning medicines and health remedies, as well as health systems, that I cannot begin to address them all, and this is not the purpose of this book. I will state that I believe all problems should be addressed with God. I am advocating we make sure we are healthy as we can be as we fight, because in many instances, the battle is over our health.

I have seen where the enemy uses our health as a

13 Lewis, C.S. *The Horse and His Boy*. HarperCollins, 1954.

weapon and causes confusion. I have friends who struggle with keeping good health, and I have friends who are hypochondriacs. The enemy will use that struggle to keep them distracted and fruitless. Can we say that all our sicknesses and diseases are attacks from the enemy? Blanket statements covering all situations cannot be applied here, but I think we should take notice of these times and seek what God is doing with them.

The hardest part about trusting God is when we know He can be the great Healer, and He isn't healing. We know He is wisdom, but we are still confused. That is when we must hold on to the knowledge that God is good, despite the evidence in front of us and the enemy whispering that God has held something good back from us. We must strengthen ourselves for this strategy when we face health battles.

As we prepare and fight, we must be aware and careful of the issue that Dr. Lloyd-Jones points out as misdiagnosing the physical for something spiritual or the spiritual as something physical. The body, the mind, and the spirit do not work independently of each other, but all dwell together in the same temple. So if one realm is down, the other two show sympathy. An example that comes to mind for women is hormones. We are well aware of the effects hormones can have on our physical and emotional health. When hormones are out of balance, the emotions and habits we already struggle with just seem to amplify. To name a few, anger, sadness, or overeating, as well as undereating, seem to spring up and take the reins. This loss of balance is a physical issue, ignited by a process of the body, but we can frustrate ourselves in trying to address it solely as a spiritual issue when our physical health is the culprit.

Another example from my own life is that I struggle with anemia. Throughout my life, I have been taking iron pills as the need required. A couple of years ago, I had been prescribed supplements to address my low iron, but blood tests revealed my iron level was at an acceptable rate. My doctor advised me to rest from taking the strong iron pills. I would still include foods high in iron in my diet, but no supplements. However, close to half a year later, I felt sluggish, unmotivated, and irritable. I began the iron supplements again, and within days, I was running through my to-do list with a much more pleasant mood. Without the supplements at the time, I was being slothful and angry, and could have labeled these as a spiritual failing. However, for this case, my physical body simply needed more iron, and I dealt with the physical need first.

Health of Spirit

Preparing ourselves spiritually is another battle on another front. We toil not just to believe in God but to believe God. We have to know Him to believe Him, so how does one get to know God? The common answer is to study His Word, join a church, serve God with others, and pray to God. This makes it seem easy. If that's all that is needed to get closer to God, then why do these actions take all we have to carry out? We study His Word, but we don't understand and misinterpret it. We try to find a church, but we don't like many, and when we do join, we find humans being imperfect humans. We serve God with others, but soon, life and misunderstandings get in the way. We pray to God, but our requests are not answered as we wanted, or we feel they get ignored. And even the highest fire in a new believer, no matter what age, dies down.

If you begin to try to find out why your prayers aren't being answered, long lists of possible reasons are given. So many books have been written about prayer over the past several centuries, and we still keep trying to figure it out. Reasons include such possible blocks to our prayers, such as: forgiveness of sins; forgiveness of others as we have been forgiven; leaving the altar to go make things right with someone; and loving your spouse. These reasons are given in Scripture. Or there might be something we missed in the past, or the next layer of forgiveness revealed that needs to be addressed. We are never done with working to be more like Christ, and just when we think we peeled off an ugly layer and should be able to improve, we are able to see the blemishes in the layer underneath.

I've prayed for many people in the past, but praying for this person at this point in my life was different. I was more aware of the hostilities this time, and I felt behind in the battle. By the time I had my eyes and ears open, the enemy had already gained much ground. I tried to find answers in books about prayer, and nothing I read seemed to fit my questions. The more I tried to find the answer, the bigger the hole I was digging. Frustrated, I would cry angry tears and ask, "What am I missing?" And I was shown that I wanted answers more than I wanted God. I wanted His knowledge and wisdom more than I wanted Him. I cannot have any of these things without Him. And in that, I missed the forest for the trees. In studying His Word, I failed to see Him for what I wished His Word said to me. In going to church, I failed to see Him for what I wanted the sermon to say to me or what worship songs they were singing. I wanted the sermon to give me the answer, not God himself. While serving God and others, I failed to see God as I focused on whether I felt helpful or liked my task. While praying (if I prayed), I failed to see God as I focused on doing prayer the right way and getting the answer I thought would be best. Instead of trusting and obeying, I failed to see Him as I struggled to be perfect, be good, and not sin.

Training

How do we prepare and train by readying ourselves for battle?

As we advance and defend the kingdom of heaven on this earth, we will be using everything we have been given. Our talents, our bodies, our situation, and our location are all gifts to be used for His purposes. As much as we can and as we are called, we work to keep ourselves ready. If an issue presents itself within our mind, body, or spirit, how can one decide which has the issue? The good news is we don't have to decide by ourselves. This takes

God's wisdom, discernment, and guidance. Start by praying for the Holy Spirit to reveal where to start and what should be done.

In getting ready, we have to keep wrestling, struggling, praying, and taking all our struggles to Him. My personal recommendation is journaling. When you reach a struggle, write about it. I've read where some people write a letter to God. I just write and keep writing whatever comes to mind. Do not stop, do not edit, just write. This is called free-writing, as I mentioned before, and this reveals feelings and thoughts you didn't know were hiding. Then you can lay them down before God and address them with Him.

PRAYER

The Lord my Shepherd, You are our Consuming Fire. Forgive us and convict us of the times we push against Your preparation for the purpose and role You have created for us. Convict us when we complain and grumble against You and Your leaders as we strive to advance Your kingdom. We must have Your wisdom, discernment, and guidance as we battle the health of our bodies. Thank you for the comfort and encouragement You send to us when we need it and give us the courage to ask for more.

CHAPTER 7

EQUIP FOR BATTLE

In Ephesians chapter 6, Paul describes the armor of God given to us to stand our ground against the adversaries. Paul wrote these verses while in prison, chained to a Roman guard. So, imagine Paul writing this part of the letter using the armor of his guard as inspiration.

The armor and each piece listed have been discussed and analyzed greatly in sermons and commentaries over the centuries. One can get lost in analyzing and searching for Paul's meaning in how he phrases each piece of the armor. To be honest, I've struggled with understanding how to apply the meaning of these verses concerning the armor of God in my own life. There is so much to learn about why Paul paired up the attributes with a certain piece, and I get bogged down in the details. I am not sure that was Paul's intent, as he used the physical functional parts of the armor of the Roman soldier to explain our spiritual protection. I have been limping along with how to apply this analogy of God's for years, feeling the importance, but convinced I was not grasping Paul's full meaning. As I studied the passage this time, the Spirit helped me appreciate how the pieces of armor correspond with the body.

A soldier relied on his armor to help protect him beyond where his skills reached. From the way armor was made, detailed and decorated back in Bible times, we can reason that it was a soldier's wearable trophy. In 1 Samuel chapter 17, Goliath's armor is described in great detail. How much it weighs, what materials it's made of, and all the weapons included. Several verses of God's Holy Word are dedicated to describing the giant's physical armor. This is the enemy's armor, and he was proud of it. It was his badge of honor to be wearing such armor, showing what a great soldier, fighter, and champion he was for his country and his king. Do we think of the gift of God's armor as an honor to wear? How do we wear our armor if we even put it on?

And why must we wear spiritual armor at all? Exodus 14:14 (NIV) tells us, "The Lord will fight for you; you need only be still." This is true for the situation the Israelites found themselves in when the Egyptians, in full armor, were chasing them. Each struggle is different, as many of God's people were called to fight. We are also given a part in our battles. Our contribution is not always to sit on the hillside and watch David go out to meet Goliath as the Israelite soldiers did in 1 Samuel 17. Many times in the battles described in 1 and 2 Kings, the Israelite soldiers still had to march out. And with some battles, the soldiers were called to fight. Joshua and the Israelites still had to march around Jericho and not wait at camp for God to bring the walls down. When the walls crashed, they still leaped over the rubble from the massive fallen walls and fought the people of Jericho. If we find ourselves in a battle, then it might be time to wear our own armor and find where the problem is. If we do not stand against the enemy, we will find ourselves standing with the enemy on the ground he just acquired.

There are responsibilities with receiving this armor. We have to choose to wear this armor, we have to practice using and testing this armor, and we must upkeep this armor. They tried to put King Saul's armor on David before he met with Goliath, but he declined. David reasoned he had not tested Saul's armor, not that the armor didn't fit. He goes into battle without physical armor, only spiritual armor. If holes and rips appear with use or disuse, I can't imagine this maintenance not being part of our work and responsibility of receiving the armor in the first place. Our talents must be developed and used; why would our armor be any different?

Paul listed the physical armor pieces to match our spiritual armor pieces in Ephesians 6:11–18. The physical armor pieces are listed in Ephesians in the following order: the belt, the breastplate, shoes, shield, helmet, and sword. Why this sequence? *Ellicott's Commentary for English Readers* offers a theory for the order in which the armour of the Roman soldier was actually put on. First the belt and the corselet, which met and together formed the body armour; then the sandals, next the shield, and after this (for the strap of the great shield could hardly pass over the helmet) the helmet itself; then the soldier was armed and only had to take up the sword and the spear. It is curious to note the spear (the pilum of the Roman soldier)- exactly that part of his equipment which, when on guard within, would not likely to assume.[14] If that's the order one would put on physical armor, maybe one should address our spiritual armor in the same manner.

The spiritual armor listed in order as it corresponds to the physical armor would be as follows: truth, righteousness, the gospel of peace, faith, salvation, the Holy Spirit, and the Word of God. These are all things Christ is Himself, and they are given to us as gifts if we take up our cross and follow Him. As I've prayed for insight into using the pieces of armor, I've been led to the following verbs for each piece: receive, test, use, and upkeep. I must receive each piece from Jesus as Paul describes in Ephesians 6, test each piece through my trials as David learned in 1 Samuel, use each piece in daily physical living referred to by Paul in Ephesians 6, and perform maintenance and keep in good condition, which I learned from Goliath in 1 Samuel 17. Simple and doable, right?

Belt of Truth

As mentioned before, the belt is what keeps the armor working as a unit. In a similar fashion for the spiritual

14 "Ephesians 6:14 - Verse-by-Verse Bible Commentary." *BibleHub*, BibleHub.com, https://biblehub.com/commentaries/ephesians/6-14.htm.

armor, the truth is what holds righteousness, peace, faith, and salvation in collaboration. Earlier, in Chapter 6, I discussed how the body, mind, and spirit all work together, and how one thing out of balance can cause great stress on the others. So any part of spiritual armor that has a twist in it will cause distress in others. And guess where the enemy is going to strike? The fiery darts are unmercifully aimed straight for the piece, already out of balance and causing havoc.

The word *truth* has brought about a discussion among Bible scholars and commentators. I've read several of these commentaries (Elliot's, Matthew Henry, MacLaren's Expositions, Benson's) as well as looked up the original Greek word using the Lexicon and Strong's Concordance about the meaning of the word *truth* used in verse 14. Almost every commentator leaned towards the word *truth,* meaning sincerity or truthfulness in this context. Benson's Commentary reasoned, "...not only with the truths of the gospel, but with truth in the inward parts, without which all our knowledge of divine truth will prove but a poor girdle in the evil day."[15] Ellicott's Commentary explains the word *truth* used here as "absolute sincerity and transparent truthfulness may well be regarded as the girdle which encloses and keeps secure every other Christian grace and virtue."[16] Christ was the truth Himself. He did

15 Benson, Joseph. "Ephesians 6:10 Commentaries: Finally, be strong in the Lord and in the strength of His might." *Bible Hub*, 1857, https://biblehub.com/commentaries/ephesians/6-10.htm. Accessed 31 July 2024.

16 Ellicott, Charles John. "Ephesians 6:10 Commentaries: Finally, Be Strong in the Lord and in the Strength of His Might." *Bible Hub*, 1905, https://biblehub.com/commentaries/ephesians/6-10.htm. Accessed 31 July 2024.

not avoid the truth to spare hurting others' feelings, offending them, or making them angry. He confronted what the occasion called for with tact and grace, but he could also cut straight to the bone. He did flip tables when He found that the Israelites had turned God's Holy Temple into a shady business center. Christ was not pretentious, sanctimonious, or false.

I am going to stay on truthfulness more than the others listed because I continue to see this come back to trouble us believers as we try to be Jesus' light in the dark and be the salt of the earth. I have a very diverse range of friends, and the unbelievers among them were raised in churches. Now, they want nothing to do with God, Jesus, or the church. Some reasons they give are just excuses, but I do pay attention to what they are saying. I believe our insincerity is a stumbling block, not just for unbelievers, but also for us as believers. We can find ourselves in a battle because we have been insincere and untruthful. The only way to fight is by being honest and confessing our true heart. Not only to ourselves, but most importantly, God. He already knows, He's not surprised, and He will not be mocked. Just as we confess sins that He already knows, he already knows the games we play with ourselves, too.

We can receive truths of the gospel and wave them as our banner, but if we misapply this to our own souls, the banner has lost its meaning and is just another flag. If there's one complaint about the American Christian Church and Christians constantly leveled at us, it's our hypocrisy. Our not being honest and truthful even with ourselves, much more God, leaks out of our pores and stinks our robes of self-righteousness that every unbeliever can detect with the accuracy of a bloodhound. What good is our righteousness, a gift from Christ Himself, or the gospel or faith, if we are unable to admit our lack of trust in God, our lack of belief that prayer works, our claims that God is good? Meanwhile, we are putting on a show, singing in church, and then cussing out the parking attendant in an effort to arrive before the other denomination crowds at the restaurants. Then, we are obnoxious and condescending to the wait staff. Do we sit in the church, say we believe in God, sing out worship songs, raise our hands, and cry? What does this mean to God if our actions say otherwise outside of church? We are fooling no one except our own selves. Don't be a church-goer, be a follower of Christ. And Christ was honest.

There could very well be some great justifications for why we struggle with being sincere. I won't be able to review all of our possible reasons, but I'll list the ones brought to my attention. Several of my friends grew up in an abusive home or with parents who showed narcissistic tendencies. Through no fault of their own, they have grown up to be people pleasers and will lie and change personality, as well as values and views, so they please a certain person at that moment. To receive love and approval at that moment is the most important thing. When I see this happen in my presence, I then wonder if they are honest and sincere with me. I ache for my friends as I watch them interact with others, denying who they are and what they value to gain the temporary reward of someone thinking highly of them. They will say and do whatever is necessary, including betraying another person, in order to please someone else. I would love for us to be open about how disingenuous this comes across to others. Feeding the bottomless well of attention and love from others will leave one hungrier than before and make you seem insincere as well as untrustworthy. We must get our worth and approval from God, and this takes an intentional effort of prayer.

The inability to be sincere, genuine, and truthful to God for the sake of appearing to be good to others, especially the unbelievers in our lives, is giving up ground to our enemy. It's a lie, whether the lie is to someone else or yourself. Lying is one of the sins listed in those Ten Commandments that everyone, including unbelievers, knows. Lying is our enemy's trait. We must equip ourselves with honesty in all we say and do. This sounds easy, just fix our own selves and stop lying, but if it were that easy, we wouldn't be going over this to begin with. I don't think we are aware of how insincere we have actually become in the quest to be polite, accommodating, appear to be a nice Christian, and not struggle with anything because Jesus is our everything. If this is a habit and integrated into your personality, start with help from the Holy Spirit. Ask Him to convict you or nudge you when you are in the process of doing this. He will give you the words to say if that's your struggle, or when to simply keep the mouth closed. This takes practice, so do not give up when it's awkward.

In addition, another help is to notice what annoys you and angers you about another person, whether a friend or not. This one will really hurt, because we judge others for what we are ourselves. One of my acquaintances has a negative outlook, and I find myself gritting my teeth at her constant critical statements. Then I realized I wasn't any better and suffered from negativity, and had to work on what came out of my own mouth. I'm still working to believe, think, and speak life instead of death.

If you struggle being honest with God and/or yourself about the way you actually feel, I want to encourage you by telling you about my recent encounter of being sincere with God. I did not get struck by lightning or zapped out of existence, and in fact, I feel God's presence now more than I ever have. One morning, I was reading a devotion on a Bible app, and it was talking about how encouraged they were that God was with them. I felt an anger fire up inside me, and I closed the devotion, beyond irritated. I was surprised I was seething, but I just went to get ready for the day. I could feel the Holy Spirit nudge me to stop and address why I was angry. I kept it all in for a minute, and I could feel the Holy Spirit just waiting, like a teacher waiting for an answer. I finally uncorked the bottle and admitted, "I'm sorry, but so what? So what that God is with me in my trials? That plant in the corner is with me, too, and it does nothing. My stuffed teddy bear was with me throughout my childhood, and it did nothing, offered no comfort or insight, but it was with me. So, forgive me, but so what? I simply do not understand how His presence is supposed to make me feel better if He does nothing in the process?" I brought to the surface a deep, deep wound from my childhood, and now it could be addressed with my God to bring healing. Was the healing immediate? By no means, but over the next several weeks, I was slowly shown in specific and personal ways what His presence meant.

Breastplate of Righteousness

The definition of "righteousness" according to *Thayer's Greek Lexicon* includes two parts: "the condition acceptable to God" and "the way in which man may attain to a state approved of God." For a little more clarification, Philip Wijaya, a contributing author at *Christianity.com,* defines righteousness as "the quality of being right in the eyes of God, including character (nature), conscience (attitude), conduct (action), and command (word). Righteousness is, therefore, based upon God's standard because He is the ultimate Lawgiver (Isaiah 33:22)."[17]

All of Isaiah chapter 11 prophecies about the Messiah and in verses 4 and 5 (NIV), righteousness is attributed to Him: "He will not judge by what he sees with his eyes or decide by what he hears with his ears; but with righteousness he will judge the needy, with justice he will give decisions for the poor of the earth. He will strike the earth with the rod of his mouth; with the breath of his lips he will slay the wicked."

17 Wijaya, Philip. "What Is Righteousness? Bible Meaning Explained." *Christianity.com*, 16 Dec. 2019, https://www.christianity.com/wiki/christian-terms/what-is-righteousness.html. Accessed 26 May 2024.

Benson's Commentary writes, "Perhaps the apostle, in this passage, alluded to Isaiah 59:17, where the Messiah is said to have put on righteousness as a breast-plate; that is, by the holiness of his conduct, and his consciousness thereof, he defended himself from being moved by the calumnies and reproaches of the wicked. No armour for the back is mentioned; we are always to face our enemies."[18] When we are putting on our breastplate, we are doing as our Messiah has modeled in a prophecy.

The breastplate covers the chest area that houses the heart, which pumps blood through our system and keeps us alive. The belt is connected to the breastplate and gives the soldier the proper fit. Righteousness covers our spiritual heart, which is kept alive with Jesus' blood moving through our actions and our lives, keeping us spiritually alive. If our heart fuels all we do and say, then it must be protected by the righteousness of Jesus Christ.

There is no way we are able to reach this righteousness by ourselves. It has to be given to us. This is what we receive. Righteousness in our lives will include living with integrity, virtue, purity of life, uprightness, correctness of thinking, feeling, and acting. Integrity and purity include truthfulness and sincerity. Righteousness will be tested as the small things opposite, such as gossip, slander, living a double life (there's truth again), spring up against us to live righteously. And again, maintenance of righteousness will be asking the Holy Spirit where in your life there is no

18 Benson, Joseph. "Ephesians 6:10 Commentaries: Finally, Be Strong in the Lord and in the Strength of His Might." *Bible Hub*, 1857, https://biblehub.com/commentaries/ephesians/6-10.htm. Accessed 31 July 2024.

righteousness and working that out with Him.

Maybe the protection we put on our heart must pass through the righteousness test. Do the things we listen to and watch pass what God would want us to listen to or watch? Because they will influence our thoughts and actions. He knows they will and warns us to keep from them. Do these pass the Philippians 4:8–9 test? Are they true, noble, right, pure, lovely, admirable, excellent, or praiseworthy? Shows that are more dramatic and include lying, treating each other horribly, gossiping, or tearing each other down are very popular and easy to watch.

According to the earlier definition, righteousness includes our conduct and attitude. We can act a certain Christian way and make a great show at it, but it's still an act. The struggle is really being who Christ wants us to be, so there is no fake act or hypocrisy. We could try applying this to how we drive in traffic. Driving the limit of the speed posted and not going around a long line of traffic and cutting back in at the last minute might be some guidelines. Not calling someone an idiot because they pull out in front of you and proceed to go under the speed limit. I'm not saying these are easy, I'm just saying they would be good examples of how to act in a condition acceptable to God. It's not just limited to refraining from doing the wrong thing, but helping others. We should let others merge, even the big semi that's going to slow us down and block our view. With our friends and family, we lift them up with encouraging words instead of being critical. Forgiveness, not giving the silent treatment, holding grudges, or being insulting, are not easy in the slightest. But this is the hard part—the application of God's way to our lives.

Shoes of the Gospel of Peace

During my research on what exactly Paul meant by this piece of armor, I found that the phrase concerning "...your feet fitted with the readiness that comes from the gospel of peace" has scholars and commentators struggling to translate what exactly Paul intended (Ephesians 6:15, NIV). *Ellicott's Commentary* stated that even the Greek interpreters found this phrasing obscure. As there is confusion among the experts, we will just keep our focus on the spiritual gift of the gospel of peace.

MacLaren's Commentary about this portion of the verse brings the point,

> ...the Gospel brought peace, and was the only thing that did, as the singular emergence of that idea that the Gospel was a peace-bringing power, in the midst of this picture of fighting. Yes, it brings both. It brings us peace first, and then it says to us, 'Now, having got peace in your heart, because peace with God, go out and fight to keep it.' For, if we are warring with the devil we are at peace with God; and if we are at peace with the devil we are warring with God. So the two states of peace and war go together. There is no real peace which has not conflict in it, and the Gospel is 'the Gospel of peace,' precisely

> because it enlists us in Christ's army and sends us out to fight Christ's battles.[19]

For many years, I have considered peace to mean lack of conflict. As MacLaren said in his commentary, no conflict whatsoever is not possible on the spiritual level. As we live, purchased and saved by Jesus, we will not have peace within ourselves as our own nature and will wrestle with what we should do as. Paul says this in Romans 7:18, "For I know that nothing good dwells in me, that is, in my flesh. For I have the desire to do what is right, but not the ability to carry it out." Our only peace is spiritual peace from the wrath of God, appeased by the sacrifice of His only Son, Jesus. When we have peace with God, we are trained and better equipped to meet our struggles because we are not focusing on calming the troubled heart.

Peace with God in my life is resting in the fact that He loves me and is for me. Getting here has taken constantly being in the Word and intentionally looking for God and who He is in His Word. I can put on these shoes and be ready to do what God calls me to do. When doubts and questions come to attack this peace, I will take these attacks to God and address them with the Holy Spirit.

Shield of Faith

Our trust in the character of God and the character of Jesus is called faith. We believe that They are who They say

19 "Ephesians 6:15 Commentaries." *BibleHub*, BibleHub.com, https://biblehub.com/commentaries/ephesians/6-15.htm.

They are. I have always found telling ourselves and others to "just trust God" is unhelpful. The question "How?" jumps into my brain when someone says that. I can't just willpower myself into a heart issue. Yet we try to use and maintain our trust in Him on our own strength. This might work for a little while, but then we criticize ourselves and become discouraged when our strength fails. The father who brought his son to Jesus for help with seizures in Mark 9:24 cries out, "I believe; help my unbelief." The father realized his belief only went so far, and he needed help to believe Jesus with his soul. We must turn to Jesus for help with the places in our hearts where unbelief still dwells.

In the beginning of Matthew chapter 18, the disciples are discussing who is the greatest in the kingdom of heaven. Jesus calls a little child to Him and sets the child in the middle of the disciples. In verse 3, Jesus says, "Truly, I say to you, unless you turn and become like children, you will never enter the kingdom of heaven". The word *converted* is further defined as turning from the curse of conduct, switching direction. We were headed towards hell, and we have switched directions and are headed for heaven by following Christ to the eternal prize. Here in verse 3, He redirects the disciples' attention from who will be in the top hierarchy in heaven to focus on making sure they get to heaven.

Helmet of Salvation

Just as the breastplate of righteousness was mentioned and put on by the Messiah prophesied in Isaiah 59:17, so was the helmet of salvation. Paul could have been referring to this scripture as he wrote this. However, the Greek words Paul wrote for this piece of armor make it different from the other pieces. First, Paul uses the word *take* and not *put on*. This word *take* is defined as to take hold of or receive.[20] Paul also uses the word for salvation differently in this phrase. Paul uses the adjective form of *salvation,* not the noun. Rewording this could be said as the salvation helmet, maybe the saving helmet, or the delivering helmet. We are to receive this helmet in the hope of the future deliverance from spiritual death into spiritual life with God.

I cannot begin to presume that I know who received salvation and who has not. I can discern the fruit of the Spirit in another person's life and actions, but I am not the judge of others' hearts. I should be concerned if another is saved or not saved, and I feel that is how I will use my salvation to help others. The upkeep of salvation is believing that once I have received it, God will keep this promise. An old trick of our enemy is to make us doubt that we have been saved. This trick has been mentioned by writers from centuries ago that believers were tormented with doubts that they were ever saved, doubts they could be saved, and revisited the process of being

20 "Take." *Strong's Concordance,* Strong's Exhaustive Concordance of the Bible, #1209.

saved over and over again. We must stand firm that once we have received the gift, God will keep His promise due to His very character and not doubt His words.

The Sword of the Spirit, the Word of God

Most of why I even mustered the courage to write this book is because I have been studying the Bible and facilitating a Bible study almost every week for over two years. Having to lead one will hold you accountable for having your notes ready. What we, a small group of about four or five women, have discovered about God by studying the Bible for ourselves has been both wonderful and humbling. So much of what we have found during these years has been included in this book.

I had been reading and studying the Bible through various Bible studies, or whatever study the women's group was going through at my church. I was a youth group leader for high school girls at my church when I noticed the girls were struggling to finish some of the devotion plans they had chosen. I prayed for and received insight that the girls were bored with learning secondhand what the Bible meant and were ready to start learning how to feed themselves. So I taught them some of the methods of studying the Bible that I learned, and we would discuss what we found during our small group. Once the girls graduated from high school and went to college, I taught this to the church women who were interested in learning how to read and use the several resources scholars and commentaries have written over the past several centuries to assist in studying the Bible.

Keeping focus on what the Bible says about God is the main focus of our study. Two of our biggest challenges that we as sinful humans face are, first, to read the Bible, and second, to read the Bible without asking what the Bible is saying to "me." Our focus should be on what the Bible says and what it says about God. Embarrassingly, I did this for decades. My reading glasses, tinted with self-focus, were on and always scanning for what this passage meant to me and who I was in the passage. Me, me, me. I would think, "Oh, was this promise or blessing for me? Oh, thank You, Lord, You are so so good to me." And even though there are promises for us in the Bible, it shouldn't be our focus every time we read it. We should be looking to the One who gave the promise, to the Giver, not the gift.

There is so much to learn from the Word of God. Learning about God, who He is, who His Son is, and what They did for us helps us focus on the One True God. They are who we should love and worship. Knowing what the Bible really says and not someone else's version or cultural traditions we grew up with sharpens our sword. We are able to cut through the lies and slander thrown our way by our enemies. Having others to study the Bible with as the Holy Spirit guides us is like no other bond I've known before. And when you find some buried treasure among the verses together, it feels like you've been seen, heard, and held by God. I love this part of training.

The Holy Spirit

I know without any doubt that you and I desperately need the Holy Spirit. We are unable to fight unless He is guiding us in the battle through prayer. Some know Him and some have not leaned on Him. If you have not had much experience with the Holy Spirit, it's time to learn what you are missing. Do a word study on the verses that contain the Holy Spirit. Learn what Jesus said about Him and reach out to Him. Have you ever asked the Lord how He talks to you? I'll share the many ways the Holy Spirit talks with me—through words I could perceive coming from deep inside me, verses that leaped off the page and answered my hopes, fears, and questions exactly. He feels like a puzzle piece fitting, and an internal nudge to pay attention to something small that I might have passed over. I love it when I talk with a friend about struggles, battles, and discouragements, and then we hear a talk, a sermon, or read a passage of Scripture that addresses every concern we had discussed. I have a good friend whom He speaks to through dreams. She waits and sees if the dream comes true, and she notices what it feels like to receive a dream from the Lord. Start with simple requests, such as understanding a verse or how to respond to a friend. Like David's armor, we must test our armor before we are in a raging battle. Ask the Holy Spirit for help on how to get to know Him. Ask how to start and then wait for the answer.

Training

How can we prepare and train by equipping for battle?

As with every part in fighting battles, we must be praying and engaging with the Holy Spirit. Isaiah 11:2 lists that He is our wisdom and understanding, our counsel and might, our knowledge and fear of the Lord. If our only offensive weapon is the sword of the Spirit, which is the Word of God, then we must read, study, know, and apply it. With all the resources available, there is no excuse. Daily reading and study is sharpening the sword and preparing your equipment.

Part of receiving our spiritual battle armor is taking care of it and making sure there are no gaps, no cracks, and no holes. We must make sure it is well taken care of and worn correctly. This could be praying over each part to check for cracks and holes in understanding that might have been caused during a previous battle. If our enemies caused the rift or gap, then he will exploit and cause the problem to grow. Questions to pray over are: Do I know what each piece is about? Where in my life am I not genuine and sincere? What verses can I memorize to help me while I struggle with what I am learning? Do I think of righteousness correctly and apply it to my life? Where in my life am I not living in accordance with God's ways? Where do I think of God as anything less than who He is?

If we ask for help and insight, we will receive it. Beginnings are always awkward. Be patient and work through the awkwardness. We are not alone in our training; we are in this together with our God, Jesus, and the Holy Spirit.

PRAYER

The Lord my Banner, You are Almighty and Lord Most High,

Forgive us when we believe we do not need Your armor and struggle in our own strength. Forgive us when we are not proud to wear Your armor and fly Your banner. Forgive us when we don't test and use the armor provided and then get upset with and blame You. Forgive us when we let the sword of the Spirit, which is Your Word, stay in the sheath and rust from lack of use. Convict us of our responsibility to take up and train with Your gifts. Inspire us with ideas on how to use and test our armor as we train for battles. Forgive us and help us with our hypocrisy, showing us where our dishonesty is hurting Your kingdom. Help us to live with righteousness, not to gain heaven, but to gain You. Thank you for giving and sharing Your Spirit with us. We need Him now and always.

CHAPTER 8

STAND FIRM

Winston Churchill has been credited with the quote, "You have enemies? Good. That means you've stood up for something, sometime in your life." During World War II, Winston Churchill is best remembered for his leadership as Prime Minister through the war and rallying his nation in defiance of their enemy, led by Hitler. He would know that standing up for what was right would create enemies.

Ephesians 6:10–11 encourages us, "Finally, be strong in the Lord and in the strength of his might. Put on the whole armor of God, that you may be able to stand against the schemes of the devil." *Thayer's Greek Lexicon* defines the word "stand" used in these verses as "of one who in the midst of the fight holds his position, against the foe." We, as followers and believers of Christ, create enemies as we stand up, also. We have received and use our armor so we can stand against our adversary's schemes and plots to turn us away from God. If we accept we are now in a battle and have received our armor and weapons, how do we stand firm? We stand firm because we know what and Who we are standing for. And when we feel discouraged and unsteady, we ask for His Scripture to encourage us, and His presence to help us. Here are a few things that we stand up for.

Fight for God's Values

When I started a Bible Study, I had a little worksheet of getting-to-know-you questions for the women to fill out. Part of the questions asked what their values were. I also had the exact same worksheet to fill out for getting to know God, including what we thought His values were. No one wanted to fill out that particular part for various reasons. I can't say that before I made the worksheet, I really contemplated and wrote down what I felt God valued. Our values can be easy to figure out, but do we know what God's values are? I wrote that He wants to save the soul from eternal death and for us to be with Him forever. Your eternal life starts once you receive the promise of eternal life and are sealed with the Holy Spirit, as 2 Peter 1:3–8 talks about. Once you are saved and are following Jesus, maybe your values have changed to be like Jesus' values.

In Matthew 22, Jesus tells the parable of the wedding feast. This parable has a king sending out his servants to notify those invited to the wedding that it was time. But the people invited found reasons not to come, and the servants were treated badly and killed by some of the invited. The king sent more servants out to invite whoever they could find to come to the wedding feast, passing over the original people invited. Do we, the servants, go out and invite whoever we find to come to the wedding feast?

In the wedding feast parable, the king is the one who gives the wedding clothes and dresses them appropriately, not the servants. I believe most of the time, we have our expectations for coming to Christ for ourselves and others in the wrong order. We expect our hearts and those of other people to be cleaned up and dressed appropriately before they hear about Jesus or accept Christ. Peter gives the sequence in 1 Peter 2:1–3 and it does not match the order we usually expect. These verses call for us to put aside all malice, all deceit and insincerity and hypocrisy and envy and evil speaking. This will lead us to long for pure spiritual milk so we may grow up. Then in verse 3, Peter uses this huge IF word. Verse 3 states, "if indeed you have tasted that the Lord is good." If and only if you have experienced the Lord's goodness are you able to put aside all those things. We are only able to eradicate those feelings and actions from our hearts when we have experienced the true goodness of the Lord. Then we can desire and crave reasonable nourishment for the soul. Then we can love one another. But we continue to keep throwing rules around first. Those rules are correct, but only to the spiritually living. These rules are death to the spiritually dead. Why are we looking for and demanding spiritual life among the spiritually dead? Even we, who have all we need spiritually, struggle with cleaning ourselves up on our own, and we expect those who don't believe to be spiritually clean already. Only with Jesus are any of those steps possible. We keep insisting that it can be done with our will and without Him, and in an order that doesn't work.

Fight for Truth

Our own senses and our own understanding can sway us and lead us wrongly if we are distracted. Standing no matter what our own understanding and interpretation communicates, is standing for and standing with God for all that He is. Standing, not falling for lies and wiles. Standing for God's Word, not stumbling back or losing ground because the devil does have a reasonable point. We must not fall for the twisting of the truth and how ideas are presented to us. We can justify almost any behavior in our minds, manipulating and steering the directive to satisfy our own nature. I began paying attention to how Public Relations companies sell an image to the general public, and how well they market a narrative that is a facade. And we unsuspectingly buy what they are selling. Their ability to sell the public any image they want about a certain person is alarming and eye-opening. These PR companies just switch what virtue is highlighted or the perspective, and the celebrity or public figure becomes popular.

Fight for Victory

Jesus conquered and achieved victory over sin and death when He was crucified and resurrected. Almost every person who calls themself a Christian will say they believe that statement. But we choose not to live victoriously. We choose to stay stuck on the crucifixion and not on Jesus being resurrected and conquering. He mastered sin and death not just for Himself but for us. What does that look like for us as His disciples, His followers? How do we apply this victory in our lives when we live surrounded and affected by a broken world?

God's definition of victory and success can be so different from our definition. We define victory as top-scoring, the best, and conquering. We don't like to lose. We like the last word and mic drops, to win arguments, to render our opponent mute against our logic, annihilating their misguided ways. But I don't believe this is a victory in the war. We believe that God's glory can only be seen in a victory, in our definition of winning. Being first, being the best, being the smartest. But that's the world's definition. God can be glorified in death, in losing, in being last, in giving it all away. We just don't like it and don't see it, and therefore, don't believe it, clinging to what we think is the better way to display how powerful and wonderful God is. We avoid suffering because we believe we've done something wrong to experience suffering.

But Jesus suffered. Not only on the cross, but throughout His time on earth. And if He cares about us and has to witness all the foolish things we do and our betrayal of Him, He has to suffer even now. If we can grieve the Holy Spirit with our forsaking and betrayals, we can definitely grieve both God and Jesus. But even in suffering, Jesus was glorified in God's kingdom. Do we believe suffering and pain won't bring Him glory? Isn't that the cross? What the enemy meant for evil, God meant for good.

When we are experiencing opposition to our work and our prayers, when we are hurting and suffering, we must view this from the perspective of becoming more like Jesus Christ. He was opposed, mocked, and suffered. We must stand and trust that the opposition and struggle we are experiencing from doing God's work will bring God glory. Even and especially when the circumstances look like the opposite.

Fight to Push Back Darkness

Tyler Staton, in his book *Praying Like Monks, Living Like Fools*, explains this victory that we as followers of Christ are given. He begins the explanation with Genesis 1:26, which says the original plan was for humans to rule. Human beings were made to be intercessors participating with God in lovingly overseeing the world, set apart, bearing God's authority to rule in selfless love. In Hebrew, the same language used in Genesis 1 for rule was ascribed to kings and queens. Ruling was a royal task.

Jesus won back the role we lost and repaired the connection and communication breach between us and God. Jesus gave us back our role as intercessors. Staton continues::

> You're not Jesus. But if you are a follower of Jesus, every single time you pray, you come before the Father clothed in the robe and crown of a rul-

> er. In the eyes of heaven, you are filled with Jesus' status and standing... Prayer is the means by which we push back the curse that's infected the world and infected us. When we engage in intercessory prayer, we are loving others on the basis of heaven's resources... But what if, according to Jesus, you've never really prayed? 'Until now you have not asked for anything in My name.' ...What if you've never come before the Father, wearing the robes of the heir, carrying the standing and status of Jesus? What if you've never plundered the riches stored away in the heavenly vault? What if you've never pushed back the curse alongside God? It's already been defeated. He's just looking for intercessors to implement the already secured victory.[21]

If the curse has already been defeated and the enemy has lost its power, then how could we be stopped? If we believed our adversary and his schemes to stop us, we have given the power away and lost the ground Jesus won. Or we keep standing and praying and fighting with our Guide and Protector.

Fight to Conquer & Triumph

Romans 8:37 says, "No, in all these things we are more than conquerors through him who loved us". Matthew Henry expands in his whole commentary the phrase

21 Staton, Tyler. *Praying Like Monks, Living Like Fools: An Invitation to the Wonder and Mystery of Prayer*. Zondervan, 2022.

"more than conquerors" with: "We are conquerors: though killed all the day long, yet conquerors. A strange way of conquering, but it was Christ's way; thus he triumphed over principalities and powers in his cross. It is a surer and a nobler way of conquest by faith and patience than by fire and sword." He writes how our enemies are baffled and overcome by the courage and constancy of witnesses to the faith. Through patient endurance in our trial, we become more than conquerors, we become "triumphers". In these conquests, we lose the earthly debris but gain the heavenly treasures such as glory, honor, peace, and a crown that does not fade. We have not been separated from Christ's love but taken into endearment.[22]

Fight to Believe God

Sometimes our unbelief gets in the way of advancing God's kingdom. This isn't a new problem. There are instances of sluggishness and hesitancy in doing what God commands or struggling to get it done throughout the Bible.

In Judges 4, Israel had lost their second Judge or deliverer when Ehud died, and they again began to do evil in the sight of the LORD. So the Lord sells them to their enemy, Canaan (the country they were supposed to wipe out but didn't), and they are oppressed by Canaan for twenty years. The Israelites cry out to the LORD for help.

22 Henry, Matthew. *Matthew Henry's Commentary on the Whole Bible: Romans 8*. Bible Hub, 1706, https://biblehub.com/commentaries/mhcw/romans/8.htm. Accessed 31 July 2024.

A prophetess named Deborah was judging Israel at this time, and in verses 6–7, she summoned Barak to ask him, "Has not the Lord, the God of Israel, commanded you, 'Go, gather your men at Mt. Tabor and taking 10,000 from the people of Naphtali and people of Zebulun. And I will draw out Sisera, the general of Jabin's army, to meet you by the river Kishon with his chariots and his troops and I will give him into your hand'?". Barak tells her he will not go unless Deborah goes with him. She agrees but tells him the honor and glory of killing Sisera will not be Barak's but given to a woman. He agrees and they go, defeating the Canaanites, and Sisera is killed by a woman. Gruesome details can be found in Judges 4.

We are not told why Barak struggled with doing as he was commanded. We see clues in his reply to Deborah that maybe he didn't trust that the Lord would do as He promised. The Lord told Barak in verse 7 the exact plan, who to take and where to go, with the ending of, "I will give him into your hand". So many times in my life, I would plead for such direct instructions. Barak is given this, and he still hesitates. Even when Deborah tells him he will gain no glory or honor for the win over their oppressors, he still requests that Deborah accompany them to the battle. Maybe he was discouraged under 20 years of enemy oppression, and he struggled to trust God. Here, he was commanded by God to go regain ground, and he refused. He was no longer standing but lying down and letting the enemy keep the land. But God sent Deborah, a judge, to encourage him to believe in God again and stand him back up.

Even in our fight to believe and have faith, God will help us. He will send someone or do it Himself. In Mark 9:14–29, Jesus helps a father to stand back up to believe God. Jesus comes down from the mountain to find a crowd watching a struggle to free a little boy from an evil spirit. The father of the boy has brought the boy to Jesus to be healed of it, but as Jesus was still on the mountain at the time, the disciples tried to cast the demon out themselves. They were not able to do so. Jesus answers, "O faithless generation, how long am I to be with you? How long am I to bear with you? Bring him to me" (Mark 9:19). When the boy is brought to Jesus, the spirit immediately reacts, convulsing, causing the boy to fall to the ground, rolling around, and foaming at the mouth. Jesus discusses with the boy's father how long this has been happening. The father ends his reply with, "...But if you can do anything, have compassion on us and help us" (Mark 9:22). In the next verse, Jesus replies, "'If you can'! All things are possible for one who believes." The father cried out, "I believe; help my unbelief!" (Mark 9:24). Jesus rebukes the spirit, and the spirit leaves the boy. Several verses later, the disciples ask Jesus privately why they were unable to cast the evil spirit out. Jesus tells them that this kind or species of demon could not be driven out by anything but prayer.

In this instance, the enemy had possessed the little boy and gained ground. The boy's father struggled with belief and had no clue what to do. He brought the boy to the

Person who could help and heal his son, but Jesus wasn't there yet. The disciples had already been given authority over unclean spirits by Jesus, as told in Mark 3, and had been sent out to heal and cleanse, and cast out demons. Which means this wasn't the disciples' first or even tenth time. They weren't novices and had done this very thing before. So, who exactly was Jesus talking to about prayer? Prayer from the disciples? They knew how to do this. Was this because of the boy's father and his half-belief? Look at the conversation Jesus is forcing the father to have while the little boy is having a violent seizure in front of all of them. I am of the stance that the disciples are unable to do anything because of the unbelief of the father himself. Jesus is the only one who can address this unbelief and heal that. The father is desperate to save his son and begs Jesus for His help to do something. And I'm not trying to add to the Word of the Lord, but if I could paraphrase into the language we use, it almost seems as if Jesus is saying, "Believe it yourself and stop leaning on everyone else to believe it for you." It's when the man himself says he believes that Jesus rebukes the spirit. The man had to choose to believe that his son could be healed by Jesus.

The two stories I just reviewed are very similar. What's the real reason for the battle? Barak has lost belief in God, and so has the boy's father. They each have their own personal battle to believe God. Not believe in Him, but believe that He is who He says He is. Both Barak and the father must believe that God can and will overcome His enemies. It's almost as if they both decided they had no choice, gave up, lay down, and let the enemy have the ground. God did not leave them there and provided someone to help. This probably will happen to us, but God will not leave us there to struggle to stand on our own.

Fight Against Temptations & Sin

The reason the enemies were oppressing the Israelites and Barak in Judges 4 was because they opened the door for the enemy by doing evil and following evil ways. Well, the enemy took the invitation, walked in, and took over. We try, but we have zero control over how much evil can take. Our enemies want all of it destroyed. We can tell our enemy, "I will only give you this closet or this section of my life, but the rest I will give to God." God controls evil, and through the name and power of Jesus, we can resist evil, but I don't think we get to negotiate. God wants every part of us, but so does our enemy. When we open the back door so the neighbors don't see him at the front door, the enemy will take over the whole property. That's not God's fault. He didn't allow for the enemy to take over; we did.

Romans 6:12 (NIV) guides us, "Therefore do not let sin reign in your mortal body so that you obey its evil desires. Do not offer any part of yourself to sin as an instrument of wickedness, but rather offer yourselves to God as those who have been brought from death to life; and offer every part of yourself to him as an instrument of righteousness." God gives us guidelines and commands to keep us from this very thing and warns us to stay away.

We have to trust His commandments and His Word. We have to be aware of our tendency to bargain, and sometimes, we avoid the responsibility for the circumstances that occur because of the bargaining. Ask for conviction from the Holy Spirit when you begin the bargaining process with our enemy. Set up boundaries that won't lead you into temptation and stand behind them.

Training

Romans 5:3–5 states, "Not only that, but we rejoice in our sufferings, knowing that suffering produces endurance, and endurance produces character, and character produces hope, and hope does not put us to shame, because God's love has been poured into our hearts through the Holy Spirit who has been given to us." Our battle is not just some useless and pointless fight just for the sake of fighting. Our battle is to strengthen our relationship with God.

My Bible study group has been studying the book of Daniel. The first six chapters give a worthy example of a man who stands up for God surrounded by enemies. Daniel was a Jewish exile abiding in the land of pagan Babylon, a world power at the time. He was honest and sincere in his devotion to God, and his character was impeccable, even as he worked for the king. He was ready at all times to stand for God and God's ways. He was at peace with God and at war with the enemy. He held his shield of faith, refusing to back down, and held off the flaming arrows of accusations and traps. He received the helmet of salvation, knowing his God would deliver him. How was he able not to buckle to the culture and the pressure? Daniel and his three friends were gifted by God with wisdom and understanding. And they prayed.

If we do not know God or know Him well, it's time to begin to get to know Him. This involves not just studying the Bible or praying to Him, but experiencing Him. We've got to engage and interact with God, Jesus, and the Holy Spirit. They are not pillows resting on the couch or plants nestled in the corner of the room. They are Persons, and this is just like getting to know any person. How do we get to know each other? We listen and we talk. We ask questions and wait for the response. If we don't understand, we ask for clarification and listen to the answer. I don't care if you think that is crazy, I think you should try it. He is right there. How do you think I ever wrote this book?

PRAYER

Holy God, You are our Strength and our Saving Grace,

Forgive us when we think that the battle will all go away if we just stop. Forgive us when we become overwhelmed by our enemy and the storm he creates, and we take our eyes off of You. Forgive us when we forget the role as conquerors that Jesus won for us, and we don't push back the enemy. Guide us like You did with Daniel, as he lived in a pagan land and served a pagan king, but he never worshiped anyone but You. May we never leave you out of the training, the fighting, and the victory.

CHAPTER 9

CONTINUE GOD'S CALL

Several years ago, I went through a severe depression. The more I tried and tried to claw my way out of it, the deeper into the sadness I buried myself. I sought help from a Christian therapist, and after many sessions, she reminded me that I was given choices. As an adult, allowing events to just happen and then feeling miserably stuck when I thought there was no other alternative was my choice. Yes, things I did not ask for were beyond my control, but my response was within my choosing. Was I going to let darkness and sadness and anger take over, or as a soldier of God, stand up and say "no"? Within a few days of realizing this, my depression faded as my mindset changed its view.

After all the separating and defining the parts of the battles, we are now presented with a choice. We are not victims of a ruthless tyrant. We are always given a choice. God will not force His will and ways upon us, although that is exactly what the other side, working with our own selfish desires, would have us believe. What choices are we given? Choice number one: to stand and fight next to God, for God, and for the land He gave us. Choice number two: to back down, not fight, and go back. You are either for Him or against Him.

Stand to Resist Our Enemies

We do not have to let evil creep into our lives and take territory; we have the choice to stand up for God and His kingdom. We have the choice to choose Jesus and take up our cross to follow Him or not choose Jesus. Even after choosing Jesus, we have the choice to take up our cross or not. We have the choice to fight for Jesus or not.

We are told that if we resist the devil and resist temptation, he will flee from us. If we review all the scripture I've used concerning battles, this is what happened when the bullying tactics didn't work. The Philistines fled when David killed Goliath, and the devil fled when Jesus resisted his temptations. We have the choice to say "no" to sin and temptation, as it no longer has a hold on us if we believe Jesus and follow Him. We are given the choice to put up with it or fight it.

We must remember our calling and purpose in Christ when our enemies attempt to steal joy and attack our trust in God. Perseverance and resilience must be sought and prayed for as God's plan is found and fulfilled. This cannot be done alone, and encouragement must be sought from the Holy Spirit and other Christians.

Stand to Commune

In Mark chapter 10, verses 35–45, there is a passage where James and John come to Jesus and request to sit at His right and His left when He is in His glory. Jesus responds, "You do not know what you are asking. Are you able to drink the cup that I drink, or be baptized with the baptism with which I am baptized?" (Mark 10:38). They reply that they could. They are choosing to drink from the cup that Jesus chose to drink from. Jesus even gives them the choice. However, I believe they had no idea what the cup could possibly hold. No one knew then what the cup held but the ones who made the plan, the Triune God.

I believe that the cup Jesus was talking about was the Cup of God's wrath, as this cup is mentioned in several verses in the Old Testament and the book of Revelation. The verses that talk about drinking from the cup of wrath are found in Job 21:20, Isaiah 51:17 and 22, Jeremiah 21:15, Revelation 14:10 and 16:19. The Greek word for "cup" used for verse 38 of Mark 10 was "poterion" and was used to describe the contents of the cup or the portion which God allots.[23] We have another source in *Thayer's Greek Lexicon* describing the word "cup" as meaning "one's lot or experience, whether joyous or adverse, divine appointments, whether favorable or unfavorable, are likened to a cup which God presents one to drink," and "to undergo the same calamities which I undergo." This makes me think of when we take communion, we

23 "Strong's Greek 4221: μετανοέω (metanoeō)." *BibleHub*, BibleHub.com, https://biblehub.com/greek/4221.htm.

drink a symbol of Christ's blood from a cup. There are several symbols that communion represents, but when we take communion as a symbol of union with Jesus, do we think of drinking the portion of what God has allotted us? None of us can drink from the same cup that Jesus did and endure as He did. But this is where we choose to take the portion which God has given us, where this portion includes joyous and adverse experiences, favorable or unfavorable divine appointments.

Stand to Persevere

There is a part in Deuteronomy chapter 20 (NIV) that gives the Israelites the principles of warfare and how the priest will address the army before the soldiers engage in the fight. The chapter starts with,

> When you go to war against your enemies and see horses and chariots and an army greater than yours, do not be afraid of them, for the Lord your God, who brought you up out of Egypt, will be with you. When you are about to go into battle, the priest shall come forward and address the army. He shall say: "Hear, Israel: Today you are going into battle against your enemies. Do not be fainthearted or afraid; do not panic or be terrified by them. For the Lord your God is the one who goes with you to fight for you against your enemies to give you victor.

The officers are then supposed to go through the different scenarios that let a soldier free from the obligation of fighting. There are four: (1) Building a new house and not having lived in it yet, (2) Planting a new vineyard and not having enjoyed it yet, (3) Getting engaged and not having married the woman yet. The fourth is in verse 8 and is about being afraid or fainthearted. "And the officers shall speak further to the people, and say, 'Is there any man who is fearful and fainthearted? Let him go back to his house, lest he make the heart of his fellows melt like his own."

The choice is given to us, too. We can choose to go back before we dishearten anyone else. We can choose to go back before we infect other soldiers with our fear. The choice is to stand and join in arms with our fellow soldiers or turn around and head back. This exact scenario is shown in Numbers 13:26–33 when Israel faced this decision standing at the border of their promised land. The spies had been in the promised land for forty days and nights and came back to report before the families what they encountered. They list all that's against them as the cities are fortified and very large, the people are powerful, and the size of giants. And as their report gained traction among the people and fear spread, the exaggerations began in verses 32 and 33 (NIV), "The land we explored devours those living in it..." By nighttime, the people were weeping, grumbling against Moses, Aaron, and God. They accused God of leading them to this place so they could fail. In Numbers 14:3 (NIV), they wail, "Why is the Lord bringing us into this land, to fall by the sword? Our wives and our little ones will be taken as plunder. Wouldn't it be better for us to go back to Egypt?" And they decided they needed a new leader and would go back. Go back to Egypt. Go back to slavery and oppression. Go back to sin and death. Go back to laboring in vain.

Oh, we can go back. There is always that choice. But as lame and ridiculous as it seems that the Israelites worked themselves into a rabid, scared, and trapped animal, so it will be for us. After all God had done and led them through, returning to Egypt is such a hard idea to accept and support. Yet, we choose this constantly in our times. On this side of the story, we can see clearly how fear drove out their trust in the Lord. It's not so clear when we are the ones who are in the fight, struggling to stand our ground.

Do not get me wrong, there are legitimate reasons to be afraid. There's the fear of failure and rejection. We are afraid of being mocked and ridiculed. We are afraid we will get hurt and have pain. We are afraid of things that could harm us, such as spiders, snakes, and heights. But fear and love cannot exist together, as is stated in 1 John 4:18, "There is no fear in love, but perfect love casts out fear. For fear has to do with punishment, and whoever fears has not been perfected in love." As much as many would like to argue, fear is a choice. Love is a choice. It's one or the other when we follow Christ.

Stand to Follow Jesus

The Israelites made the choice to return to spiritual slavery hundreds of years later in the New Testament. Matthew 27 tells how the Israelites made this decision at the trial between Jesus and Barabbas. Looking further into this passage and the original Greek, we learn that each man's name once again plays a significant part. The first choice given is Jesus Christ. The second choice given is Jesus Barabbas. Yes, the notorious prisoner's first name is Jesus, too. I never knew this until a few years ago, but often, his first name is left out in many English translations. Even more interesting is the meaning of his second name, Barabbas. Notice the word "abba" in there? Barabbas means "son of Abba." Jesus was on trial for claiming He was the Son of the Father, and here is Barabbas with a name meaning son of Abba. Mark 15:7 gives the information that Jesus Barabbas was a criminal, but only to the Romans, for he had participated in a rebellion against the Roman government. This is what the Jews expected Jesus Christ to be doing as their Savior—releasing them from their physical and earthly oppressors, the Romans. They believed they had no need for a spiritual saving. They wanted results, and Jesus Barabbas brought dramatic results by participating in an insurrection against the oppressive Rome. Barabbas fought the world's way. Jesus Christ was fighting God's way. Once again, Israel chose to return to Egypt. And so can you.

Stand to Fight God's Way

God's will for how we are to fight in His army is not hidden in obscure, symbolic verses or added in a how-to section. He has clearly stated throughout the Bible, both Old and New Testaments.

Paul gives insight concerning living and fighting God's way in Romans 12:9–12 and Romans 13. The overarching theme for how to conduct ourselves at times of peace and at times of war is to love. These verses list out for us how to love others, love our enemies, and love the life God has given us. These are for every occasion and time, in war and in peace.

How to love others includes a genuine love, devotion to one another, rejoicing with those who are rejoicing, and mourning with those who are mourning, as well as sharing with the Lord's people who are in need. When we struggle to love others, we must pray and ask for help to do this. How many times have you tried to force yourself to like someone and love them the way you know we should? It might have been a fake it 'til you make it type force, but that's not a genuine love. When this happens for me, I have to confess that I am struggling to love others, and I need God's love to follow His commands. That prayer was answered.

How to love our enemies or those we feel are against us involves us blessing and not cursing those who persecute us. We are told not to repay anyone evil for evil and not to avenge ourselves, but to leave room for God's wrath. If our enemy is hungry, feed them. If they are thirsty, give them a drink. We are not to be overcome by evil, but overcome evil with good. I feel loving our adversaries is even harder than loving others. Praying and asking for God's love, wisdom, discernment, insight, and courage to overcome evil done against us by not retaliating will be intentional work. We must prepare ourselves that taking this route most likely will not bring instant results and could be long-suffering, like Jesus. Pray to be reminded when needed of Ephesians 6:12, which says we do not struggle against flesh and blood but against the rulers, powers, and spiritual forces of evil in the heavenly places.

The list for loving the life we live and are given by God starts with: despise what is evil and attach to what is good. Be joyful in hope, patient in affliction, and faithful in prayer (Romans 12:9–12). We should not be conceited or think ourselves wise for we are given wisdom by God. Do not be inactive but eager in spirit to serve the Lord. We are to submit to the control of the governing authorities, for there is no authority except from God and established by God, and walk honestly in the day, not in rioting, drunkenness, sexual immorality, strife, envy. Give to everyone what is owed to them, whether it's taxes, revenue, respect, or honor.

The books of 1 and 2 Peter, written by Simon Peter, also give us guidance on how to fight the Lord's battles without using our own ways. This disciple is the one who was called Satan, or Adversary, because he was inserting his ways to stop all that God was doing. Peter wanted to do things such as cut off an ear to stop Jesus' arrest. Yes, that disciple gives us what we need to battle in the way God wants us to in his letters found in 1 and 2 Peter. Some of his guidance overlaps with what Paul gives in Romans, such as being self-controlled and getting rid of all malice, deceit, hypocrisy, envy, and slander of any kind from our lives. Peter also advises in verse 7 of 1 Peter chapter 5 for us to cast all of our anxiety onto God because He cares for us. Peter encourages us in the following verses 8–10 (NIV),

> Be alert and of sober mind. Your enemy the devil prowls around like a roaring lion looking for someone to devour. Resist him, standing firm in the faith, because you know that the family of believers throughout the world is undergoing the same kind of sufferings. And the God of all grace, who called you to his eternal glory in Christ, after you have suffered a little while, will himself restore you and make you strong, firm and steadfast.

Stand to Worship God

There is a story in Daniel 3 of the Babylonian king making an enormous image of gold and commanding everyone to bow down to worship this image when they heard music. Whoever did not bow and worship when music was played would be thrown into a blazing furnace. Shadrach, Meshach, and Abednego were Jewish exiles living in Babylon and working in the king's service. Their co-workers told the king that these three exiles refused to pay attention to the king, nor did they serve his gods or worship the image of gold the king set up. After a brief trial where the three were given an opportunity to bow and worship the image, King Nebuchadnezzar was told in verse 16–17 (NIV) by the three Jewish exiles, "O Nebuchadnezzar, we do not need to defend ourselves before you in this matter. If we are thrown into the blazing furnace, the God we serve is able to save us from it, and he will rescue us from your Majesty's hand. But even if he does not, we want you to know, Your Majesty, that we will not serve your gods or worship the image of gold you have set up." The king was furious and had them thrown into a furnace that had been ordered to be stoked even hotter than before. These three men stood up to this powerful king and refused to bow down to any god except the Most High God. They weren't even sure God would save them, but they had no doubts He could. They faced death and were led, bound and fully clothed, into the furnace. They were not just protected but accompanied by a fourth supernatural being in the furnace with them. They not only walked back out of the furnace, but were unharmed. The fire had not touched them or their hair, their robes were not scorched, nor did they even smell of smoke. But the bonds were gone. Even King Nebuchadnezzar was praising God because they chose to stand and not bow.

Training

In the midst of our struggles and battles, there are so many reasons to stand. But we must decide to stand and fight. Our options are to choose life in Jesus or return to oppression by our enemies. There is no neutral ground. We are given advice and guidelines by many of God's warriors, examples of what to do and what not to do in battle. Most people view the Ten Commandments as the rules that determine whether we go to heaven or hell. But even these are choices.

- Choose God first, not the little gods. Following other gods brings spiritual death, and they have you doing gross and crazy things (see Leviticus). God is life.
- Do not use the Lord's name without purpose, in vain—using a powerful word and not meaning it brings God's wrath and spiritual death. The LORD's name is Life.
- Keep the Sabbath. Running yourself into the ground brings physical and spiritual death. Resting and worshiping God brings life.
- Honor your mother and father. Dishonor brings spiritual death. Honor brings life.
- Do not murder. Murder brings physical and spiritual death. Choose to give life.
- Do not take another's spouse. Betrayal brings spiritual death. Being faithful brings life.
- Do not take another's possessions. Betrayal brings spiritual death. Being faithful brings life.
- Do not lie. Lies bring spiritual death. Truth is life.
- Do not envy. Envy brings spiritual death. Encouragement brings life.

God wants us to choose Him. Don't you want others to choose to be with you, and not because you've manipulated them or forced them to be near you? How do we, made in His image, think He feels?

For further study, because I simply couldn't include it all, try 1 and 2 Peter, Ephesians, and the Gospels themselves. Romans has much more than what I reviewed. Jesus, in Matthew chapter 5 from verses 21-48, the Sermon on the Mount, and Micah chapter 6. Look specifically for emotions and actions to remove from us and what to bring in its place. As you continue to read and study the Bible, you will begin to notice more.

PRAYER

Most High God, You are our Great Reward,

Forgive us when we forget that You are the prize and our hearts chase something of lesser value. Encourage and strengthen us as only You can do, so that we continue to stand our ground for Your kingdom. Thank you for Your provisions and portions.

May Your will be done on earth as it is in heaven. And may we be the warriors that You use to make sure it is.

CHAPTER 10

CONCLUSION

I pray that you have been able to find heart and courage in these pages.

Psalm 98:4 tells us to shout joyfully to the LORD, all the earth; break forth into joyous song and sing praises! If we look up what Hebrew word is used for *shout joyfully* in this verse (and you know by now, it's one of my favorite things to do) it is *rua* and the definition is "to raise a shout, give a blast."[24] However, looking at all the other verses where this Hebrew word is used, you find this same word "rua" used in Joshua 6, when the Israelites were told to shout as they circled Jericho for the last time. Shouting joyfully to the LORD is a battle cry. Jesus had joy, and He prayed that for us in John 17:13. May we fight for His joy and refuse to let anyone steal and destroy it.

I hope you have found you are not alone, nor are you the only one finding themselves caught in a struggle after they agreed to pray, or agreed to help in ministry, or

24 Strong, James. *Strong's Exhaustive Concordance of the Bible*. Abingdon Press, 1890. Entry #7321

agreed to answer a call they believed was from the Lord.

I hope that recognizing you are in a battle and trying to find the ground you are defending and advancing has encouraged you that this battle is not in vain. The battle has meaning and purpose.

I hope you can identify your enemies and see their plays and wiles from a mile away, including the enemy within. I pray this encourages you to keep going.

I hope that identifying the battle and seeing the three levels of physical, spiritual, and eternal gives insight and discernment in your fight. I hope you are able to address the root of the battle and work on what you've found with God.

I hope as you prepare for battle, that you are prepared for what's on the other side of the fight you are going through.

I hope that seeing the equipment provided for us by God will draw us even closer to God.

I hope that as we take up our identity with Jesus Christ as conquerors, we can be ready to finish this battle and be in training for the next one.

I hope we choose to trust in God and persevere this calling and purpose in Christ. I hope we pray for and find fellow soldiers as we choose to continue our service.

David had a group of mighty men, and they are listed in 2 Samuel chapter 23. I attempted to do a study on the meaning of their names and where they were from, but after digging around and looking at several commentaries, their names and where they are from don't match the list given in 1 Chronicles 11:10–47. Therefore, it is believed that the names given were misunderstood. We therefore don't know much about David's mighty men personally, but they are counted in the Bible as mighty warriors. The mighty men included David's nephews, and some were Israelites. But many were Gentiles, outsiders, and many were even from enemy countries. Some were related to counselors who betrayed David. They were known for their bold fighting and fighting for their king and their Lord. They stood their ground when outnumbered and when all alone. They broke barriers and stayed loyal. They used weapons and their bare hands, and even used someone's own weapon to kill them. They were well-trained and ready for whatever was brought their way.

I have always been fascinated by David's mighty men and the brief one-line stories of their epic battles. I have always wanted to be fearless like they seemed to be until I was in the middle of this messy fight. Maybe these mighty men weren't so mighty at the beginning, but trained hard and soon earned the title. Maybe they took their training seriously and viewed their training to make them more effective and better warriors. Maybe they didn't spend so much energy and effort trying to get out of preparation and training. Maybe they did all the things that I won't do to become a warrior. Maybe they knew they were fighting their enemies so that others could live.

Preparation and training is not sitting and listening to a lecture about a subject we need help with. Preparation and training is hard on the body and mind, and requires practice and repetition. Any athlete who wants to improve their skill performs, listens, and applies advice and criticism from coaches and trainers, and does it again. Improvements in other areas, such as strength training and endurance runs, are also involved. Sitting and watching videos or reading books and not physically doing it will not provide improvement.

I can't be trained as God's warrior if I don't let myself be trained, involved, and trust my God. I am still in training, and I will always be in training. Complaining and grumbling when battles continue or repeat only hinders my progress and prolongs the trial. My perspective needs to be about 'what I can learn?' and not about 'when will this end?'

Our relationship with God cannot be conducted by repeated formulas. A good, healthy relationship with another person can't be maintained that way, and yet, we try that with God. God cannot be managed, supervised, masterminded, handled, guided, governed, or led. Connecting with Him can be helped through discipline, but a heartless formula of 'this' plus 'that' equals 'result' will disappoint us very soon. He enjoys our presence as Zephaniah 3:17 (NIV) tells us, "The Lord your God is with you, the Mighty Warrior who saves. He will take great delight in you; in his love he will no longer rebuke you, but will rejoice over you with singing." If you have no desire or need to be near God, then I honestly don't believe you have experienced Him, and you need to ask in prayer for that.

Even with gifts such as the Bible and Jesus Christ to

assist us, God is still so misunderstood and undervalued. Jesus tells the parable of the prodigal son to explain the love and character of our Father. In Luke 15:11–31, Jesus is using the physical kingdom, in the form of a father with two sons, to explain the spiritual and the eternal kingdoms. Jesus is also expanding our heart for Our Father.

In verses 14–19, the youngest son contemplates his worth as he sits among the defiled pigs. His thinking out loud reveals that he believes he is not worthy of his father's love, and maybe he can work to regain his worth again. This younger son had journeyed to a distant country, where he squandered his wealth in wild living. After he had spent all he had, a severe famine swept through that country, and he began to be in need. So he went and hired himself out to a citizen of that country, who sent him into his fields to feed the pigs. He longed to fill his belly with the pods the pigs were eating, but no one would give him a thing. In Luke 15:17–19, he finally comes to his senses and says, "How many of my father's hired servants have more than enough bread, but I perish here with hunger?" I will arise and go to my father, and I will say to him, "Father, I have sinned against heaven and before you. I am no longer worthy to be called your son. Treat me as one of your hired servants."

The part where the younger says, "Treat me as one of your hired servants," expresses his belief to earn favor as a servant, not given as a gift. This reveals the son's true heart towards his father. This is similar to us trying to gain salvation, eternal life, and blessings by good deeds.

We know in our head that this is not how God works, we proclaim this with words and sing all the songs. However, our actions reveal what we believe when life does not work according to our plan and timetable.

The older son is introduced in verses 25–30:

> Now his older son was in the field, and as he came and drew near to the house, he heard music and dancing. And he called one of the servants and asked what these things meant. And he said to him, 'Your brother has come, and your father has killed the fattened calf, because he has recieved him back safe and sound.' But he was angry and refused to go in. His father came out and entreated him, But he answered his father, 'Look, these many years I have served you, and I never disobeyed your command, yet you never gave me a young goat, that I might celebrate with my friends. But when this son of yours came, who has devoured your property with prostitutes, you kill the fattened calf for him!'

The older son had been talking with a servant when he learned his younger brother came back not to a closed door but to a party. Look at the accusation he levels at his father in verse 29: "These many years I have served you, and I never disobeyed." His words reveal his heart—I have served you, worked. Almost as if he is saying, "I stayed and obeyed, which means my work is good. I have worked, served, and always done the right thing, but the son who didn't and doesn't deserve anything good gets the party. Not me. Not the one who has slaved away for years and done his work obediently. Where is the reward? What is the reward?" Like the younger son, this reveals his true belief about his father. Isn't he also trying to work for his father's blessing and to be noticed and celebrated as the good son?

Isn't the older son now angry that he's been working, "serving" as he puts it, and then his younger brother rolls up at the end, having squandered the inheritance he was already given on sinful pursuits, and then, receive even more? What's the true reward for the sons? Is it the father or all the gifts he gives?

Therefore, both sons believe they have to earn their place with their father, and both have totally overlooked and misunderstood the extent of their father's grace. One rebelled in action for all to see, and the other rebelled in heart for no one to see. Neither appreciated their father for who he truly was, almost as if there was no relationship with him or love for him. Maybe these two sons see their father as a harsh and stern man. Notice the father went out to meet both of his sons where they were and loved them into his house. We know the returned sinner went in, and we are left wondering if the obligated rule-follower ever did.

We can believe the same as the sons in the parable did with our Heavenly Father. Have you ever thrown at God the question of, after all you have done for Him, why He gives you a stone? Or a snake? We work and work and do this and that and count all of our good deeds and stack them at His feet and ask why. WHY was what we received not equal to all our good deeds done? I know I certainly have. But the very last time I went to my Lord to cry about it, I could feel the Holy Spirit softly opening my ears to actually hear what I had just accused God of. This is what the human condition does well—keep track and measure in our favor. In this physical kingdom's way of banking, all our good work should earn an equal or better return. Just like Santa Claus. Just like any false god we have set up. Anything else is unbalanced, unfair, and by our banking definition, not good. This world loves this banking system because it's about control. If it's based on how much good work is done, then we can set the terms and demand what is received in return. You *owe* me a good and equal return for all my suffering, sacrifices, and work for you. But this is not our Father's way, because we can never earn the goodness He gives. His kingdom is right side up, and we're the ones who live upside down. Here we are, influenced by this world's systems that are the exact disrespectful opposite of our God's kingdom and demand God change to the bank of our self-built, little kingdom. Our Father's way is grace to the undeserving, and we are all undeserving.

We can run back to our Father and have our misguided perception of Him turned to Who He truly is. He loves us and wants the best for us. But we can get our feelings and our trust in Him hurt by our misinterpretations of His actions. God is our reward. We have to fight to believe this and not be led away to a paltry substitute.

Romans 8:31–39 (NIV) speaks of God being for us and gives us the proof that He is. I don't know about you, but sometimes in this world that seems to oppose so much of what I hold dear, I need the reminder. Paul starts with a rhetorical question, "If God is for us, who can be against us?" Who can oppose us if God is with us? God did not spare His own Son from His wrath and death, so that we are spared from His wrath and death. God delivered His Son up for us all. God freely and graciously gives us all things because of His Son. Paul continues with more rhetorical questions—Who can bring a charge against God's elect? Who is the one that condemns? Who will separate us from the love of Christ? The answer is no one. Because in verse 37, "in all these things we are more than conquerors through him who loved us."

www.ingramcontent.com/pod-product-compliance
Ingram Content Group UK Ltd.
Pitfield, Milton Keynes, MK11 3LW, UK
UKHW042020290726
14061UKWH00002BB/103

9 798891 852297